Piano • Vocal • Guitar

BEST MODERN CHRISTMAS SONGS

2 **Almost There**
MICHAEL W. SMITH (FT. AMY GRANT)

8 **Christmas Always Finds Me**
INGRID ANDRESS

18 **Christmas Lights**
COLDPLAY

26 **Christmas Saves The Year**
TWENTY ONE PILOTS

30 **Christmas Tree Farm**
TAYLOR SWIFT

13 **Cozy Little Christmas**
KATY PERRY

38 **Everyday Is Christmas**
SIA

42 **For Love On Christmas Day**
ERIC CLAPTON

56 **Glittery**
KACEY MUSGRAVES (FT. TROYE SIVAN)

62 **Hallelujah**
CARRIE UNDERWOOD & JOHN LEGEND

68 **He Shall Reign Forevermore**
CHRIS TOMLIN

76 **I Need You Christmas**
JONAS BROTHERS

80 **Let There Be Peace**
CARRIE UNDERWOOD

49 **Light Of The World**
LAUREN DAIGLE

86 **The Lighthouse Keeper**
SAM SMITH

90 **Mistletoe**
JUSTIN BIEBER

100 **Noel**
CHRIS TOMLIN (FT. LAUREN DAIGLE)

106 **Present Without A Bow**
KACEY MUSGRAVES

112 **Santa Tell Me**
ARIANA GRANDE

118 **Snowman**
SIA

95 **Something About December**
CHRISTINA PERRI

122 **Underneath The Tree**
KELLY CLARKSON

ISBN 978-1-70513-915-8

T0057197

Visit Hal Leonard Online at
www.halleonard.com

Contact us:
Hal Leonard
7777 West Bluemound Road
Milwaukee, WI 53213
Email: info@halleonard.com

In Europe, contact:
Hal Leonard Europe Limited
42 Wigmore Street
Marylebone, London, W1U 2RN
Email: info@halleonardeurope.com

In Australia, contact:
Hal Leonard Australia Pty. Ltd.
4 Lentara Court
Cheltenham, Victoria, 3192 Australia
Email: info@halleonard.com.au

ALMOST THERE

Words and Music by MICHAEL W. SMITH,
WES KING and AMY GRANT

Moderate Ballad

mp

Mar-y, full of in-no-cence, car-ry-ing the Ho-ly Prince, you're

al-most there, you're al-most there. Moth-er of the Liv-ing Word,

trust-ing in the voice you heard, you're al-most there, you're

* Recorded a half step lower.

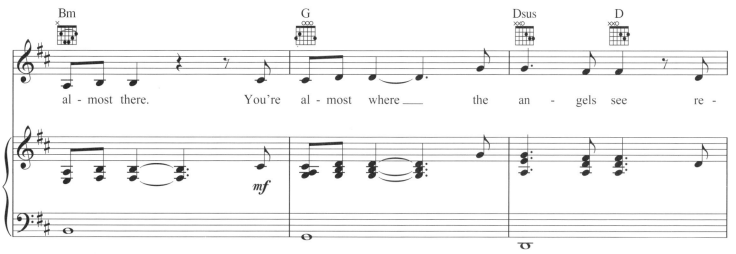

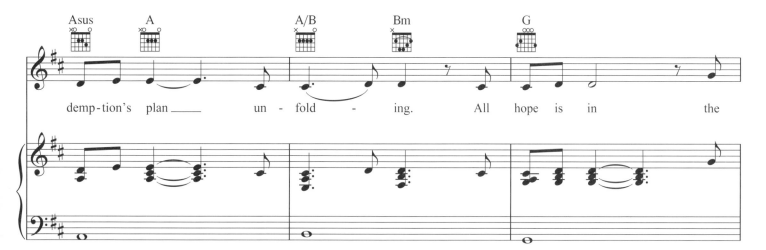

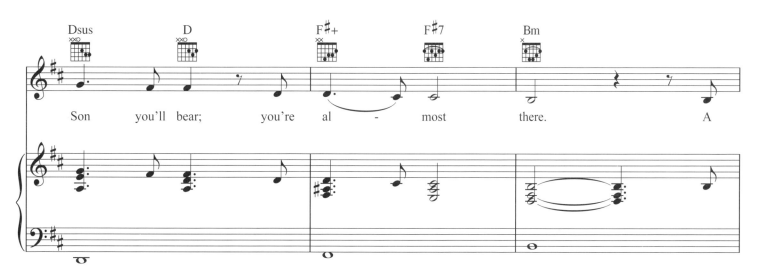

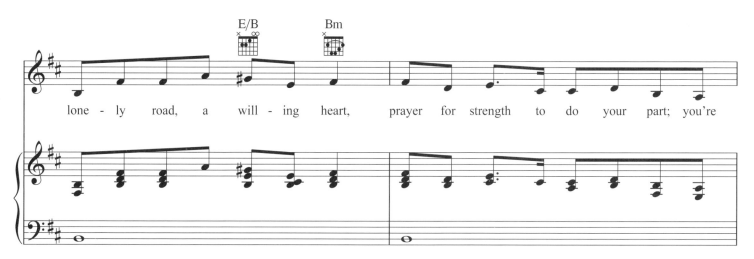

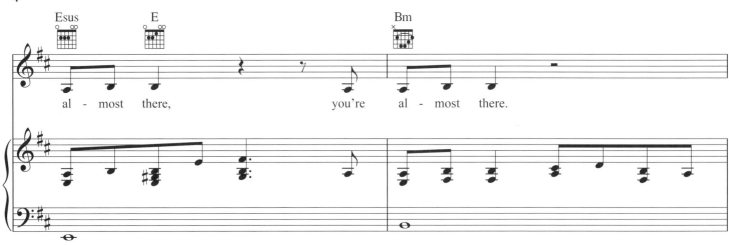

al - most there, you're al - most there.

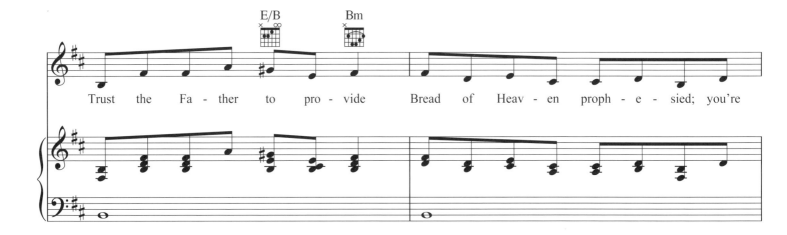

Trust the Fa - ther to pro - vide Bread of Heav - en proph - e - sied; you're

al - most there, you're al - most there. You're al - most where the

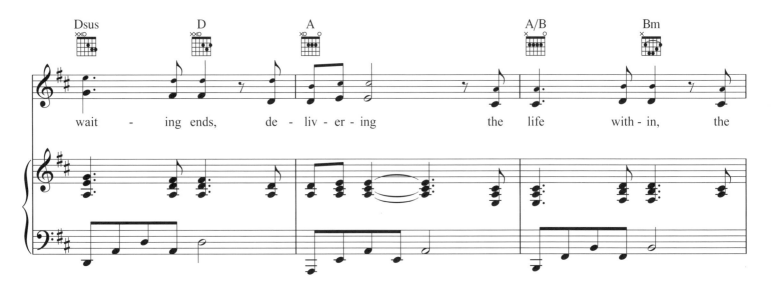

wait - ing ends, de - liv - er - ing the life with - in, the

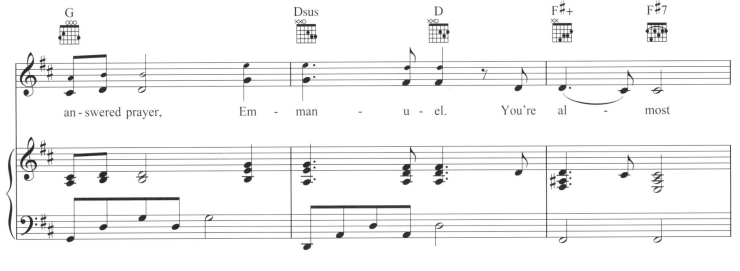

an-swered prayer, Em - man - u - el. You're al - most

there. You're al - most where _____ the jour - ney ends, where

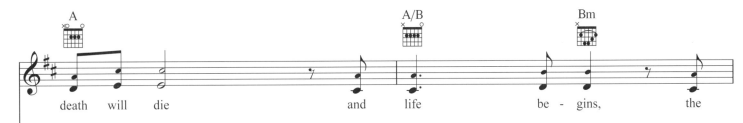

death will die and life be - gins, the

an-swered prayer, Em - man - u - el; you're al - most,

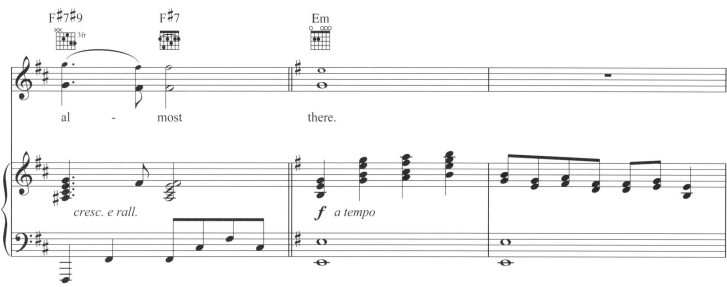

al - most there.

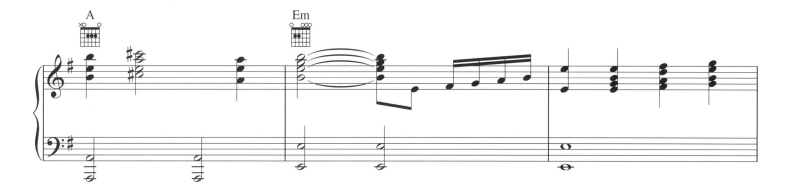

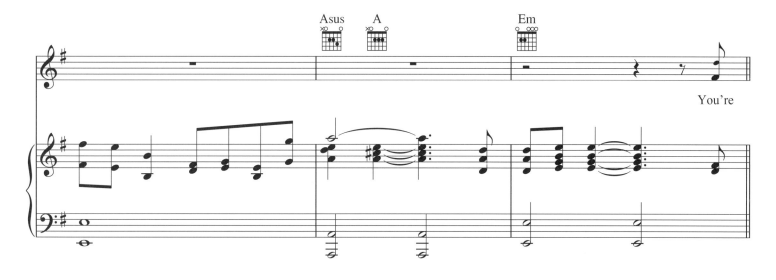

You're

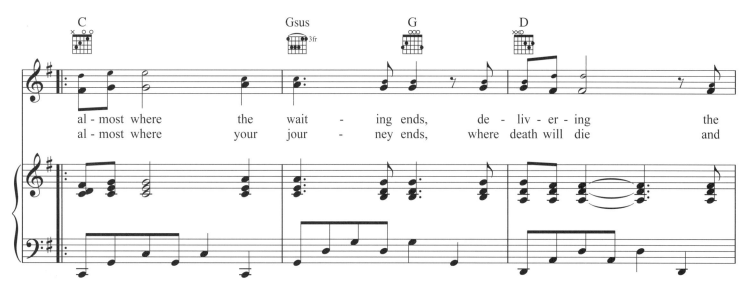

al - most where the wait - ing ends, de - liv - er - ing the
al - most where your jour - ney ends, where death will die and

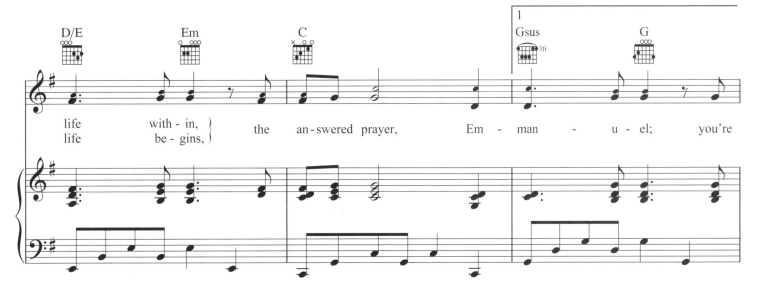

life with-in, } the an-swered prayer, Em - man - u - el; you're
life be-gins, }

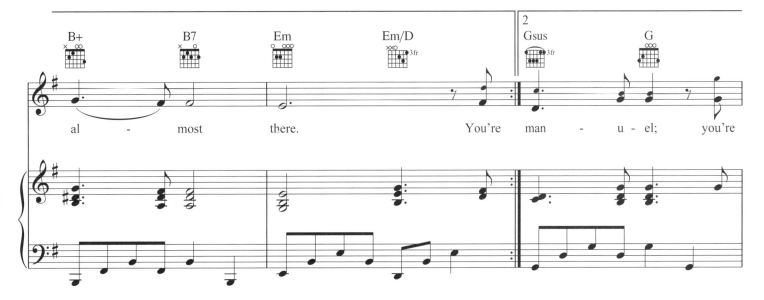

al - most there. You're man - u - el; you're

al - most there.

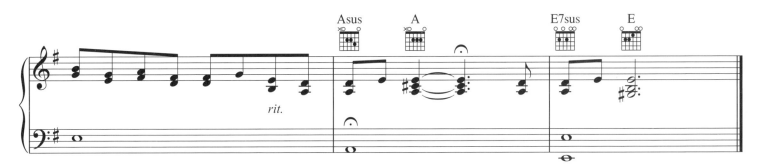

CHRISTMAS ALWAYS FINDS ME

Words and Music by INGRID ANDRESS,
DERRICK SOUTHERLAND and SAM ELLIS

Piano Ballad

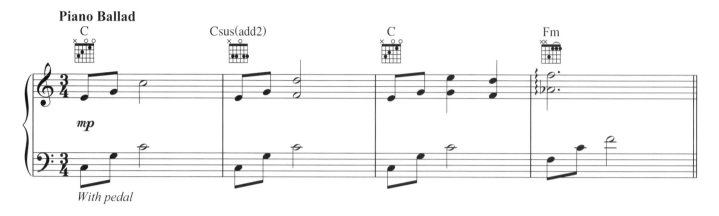

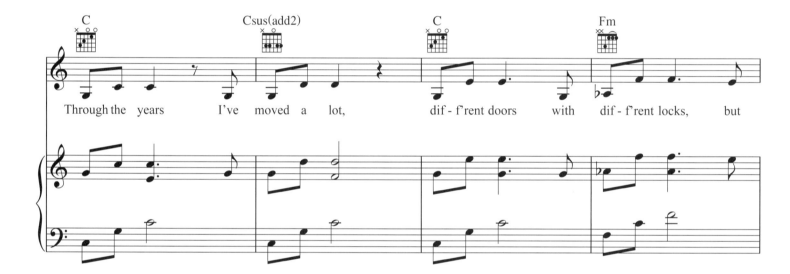

Through the years I've moved a lot, dif-f'rent doors with dif-f'rent locks, but

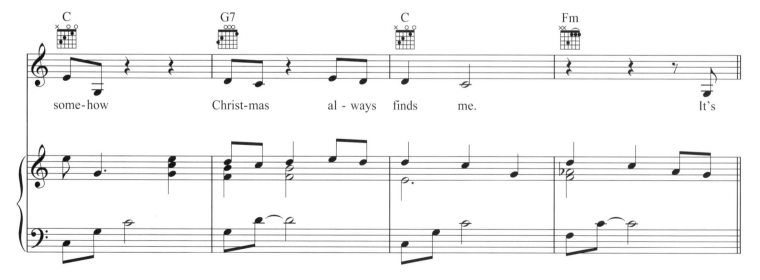

some-how Christ-mas al-ways finds me. It's

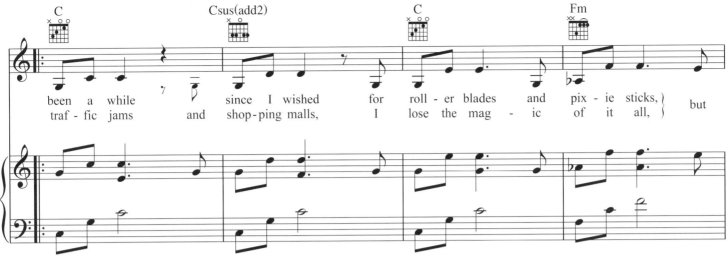

been a while since I wished for roll-er blades and pix-ie sticks, but
traf-fic jams and shop-ping malls, I lose the mag-ic of it all,

some-how Christ-mas al-ways finds me. When

"Sil-ver Bells" and "Si-lent Night" and mis-tle-toe's no-where in sight, with

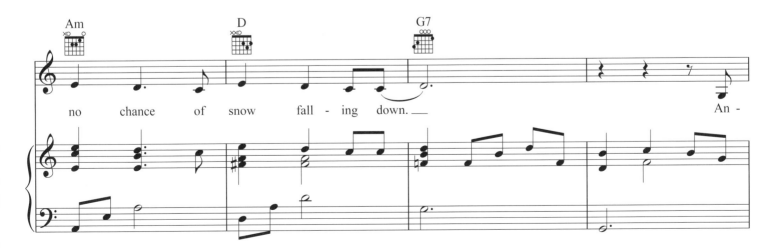

no chance of snow fall-ing down. An -

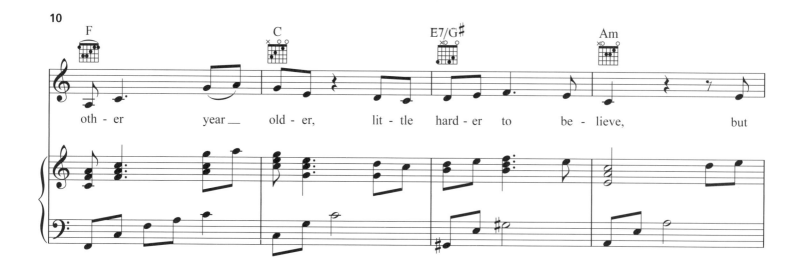

oth - er year __ old - er, lit - tle hard - er to be - lieve, but

some - how Christ - mas al - ways finds me.

In finds me. _____ It

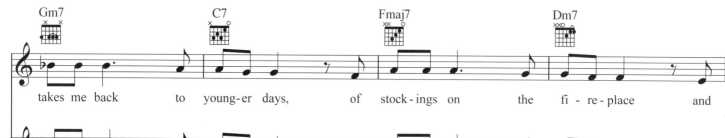

takes me back to young - er days, of stock - ings on the fi - re - place and

pres-ents stacked and wait-ing by the tree. ___ And

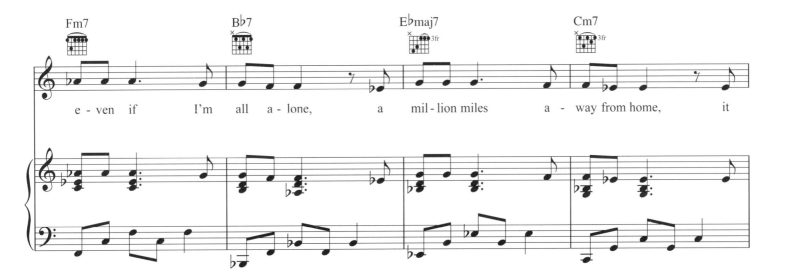

e-ven if I'm all a-lone, a mil-lion miles a-way from home, it

shows up in a warm mem-o-ry. _____

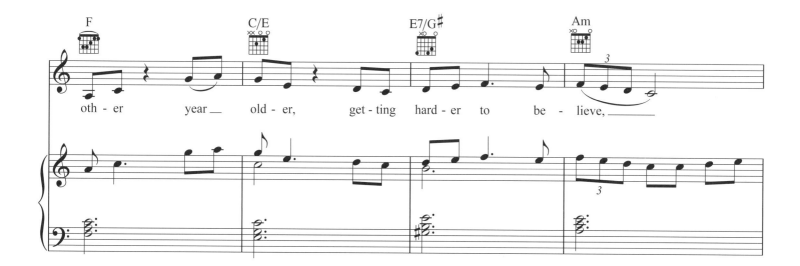

oth - er year __ old - er, get - ting hard - er to be - lieve, ___

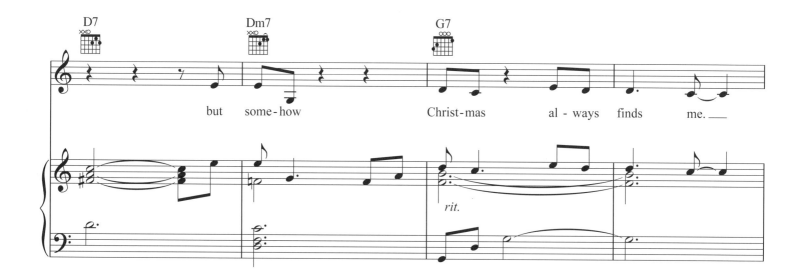

but some - how Christ - mas al - ways finds me. __

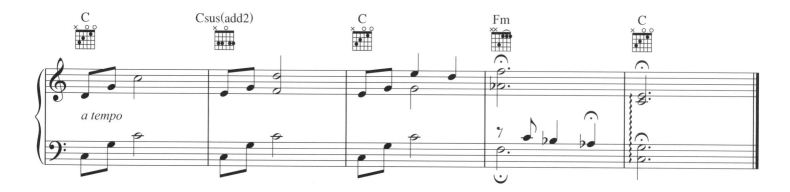

COZY LITTLE CHRISTMAS

Words and Music by KATY PERRY,
FERRAS ALQAISI and GREG WELLS

Ev-'ry-bod-y's in a
San-ta, take the

hur-ry, in a flur-ry, 'cause we've
day off. Get a mas-sage, shop-

-ping 'til they're drop-ping in the snow. A Kids are
got this one all un-der con-trol. lit-tle

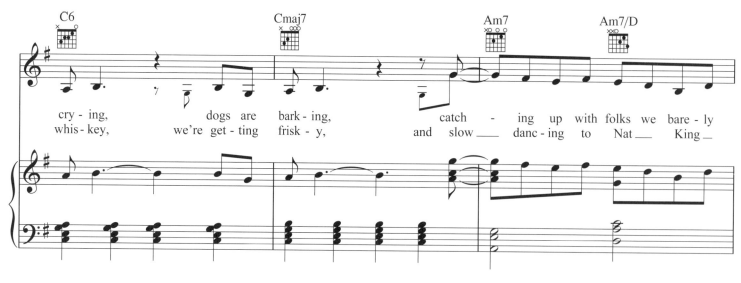

cry - ing, dogs are bark - ing, catch - ing up with folks we bare - ly
whis - key, we're get - ting frisk - y, and slow ___ danc - ing to Nat ___ King ___

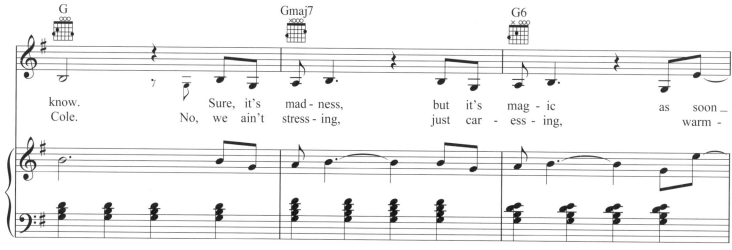

know. Sure, it's mad - ness, but it's mag - ic as soon ___
Cole. No, we ain't stress - ing, just car - ess - ing, warm -

___ as you hang up the mis - tle - toe, 'cause you're the rea - son for the
- ing up our pop - si - cle ___ toes. Noth - ing's miss - ing, 'cause you're a

sea - son. Now we _____ don't need to keep up with the
bless - ing. Yeah, you're ___ the on - ly one I'm wish - ing

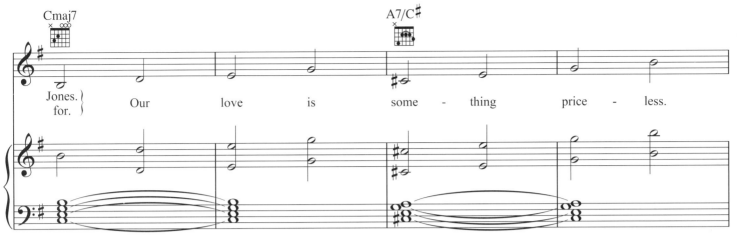

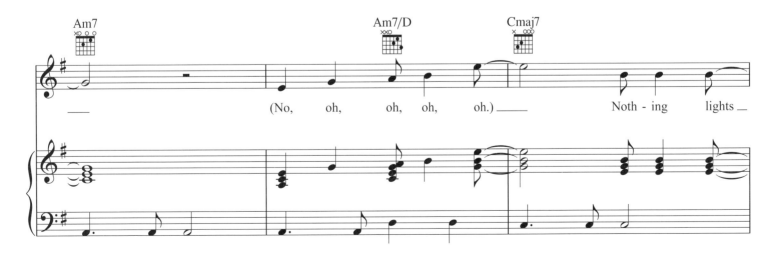

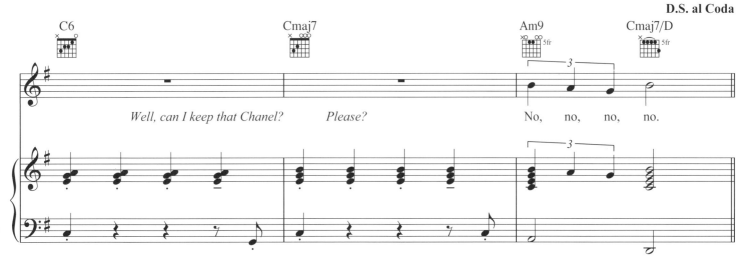

Well, can I keep that Chanel? Please? No, no, no, no.

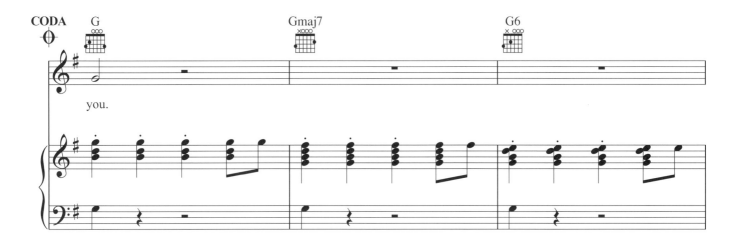

you.

Just you and me, un - der a tree,

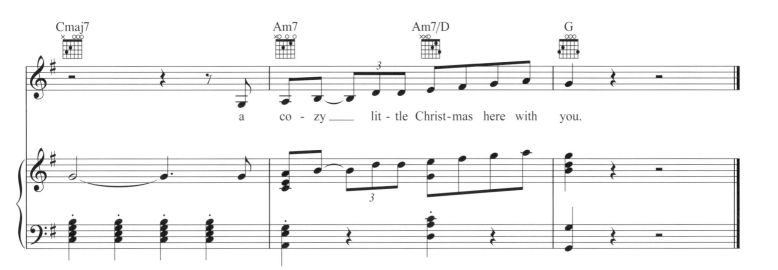

a co - zy ___ lit - tle Christ-mas here with you.

CHRISTMAS LIGHTS

Words and Music by GUY BERRYMAN,
WILL CHAMPION, CHRIS MARTIN
and JONNY BUCKLAND

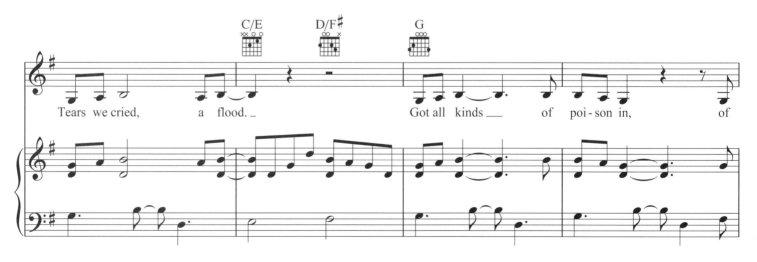

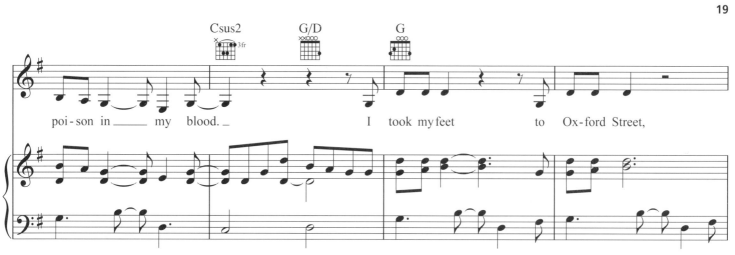

poi-son in ___ my blood. ___ I took my feet to Ox-ford Street,

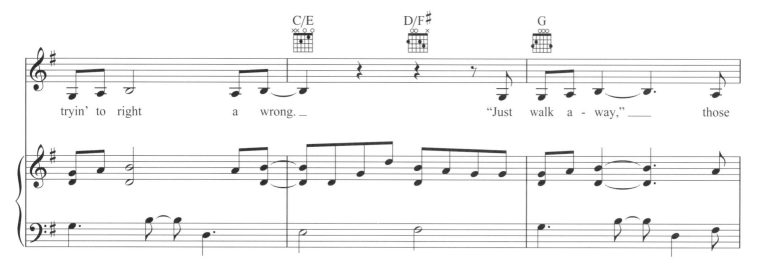

tryin' to right a wrong. ___ "Just walk a-way," ___ those

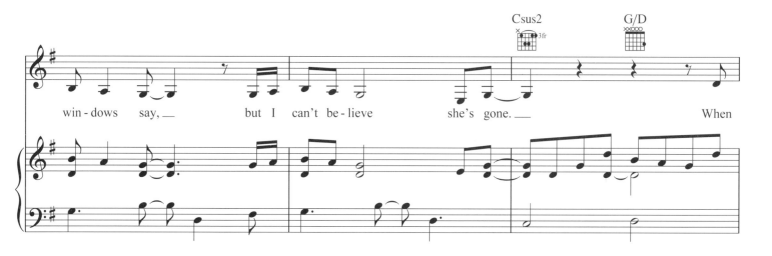

win-dows say, ___ but I can't be-lieve she's gone. ___ When

you're still wait-ing for the snow to fall, ___ it does-n't real-ly feel ___ like Christ-mas at all. ___

Up a - bove, can - dles on air flick - er, oh, ___ they flick -

er and ___ they flow, ___ and I'm up ___ here hold - ing on ___

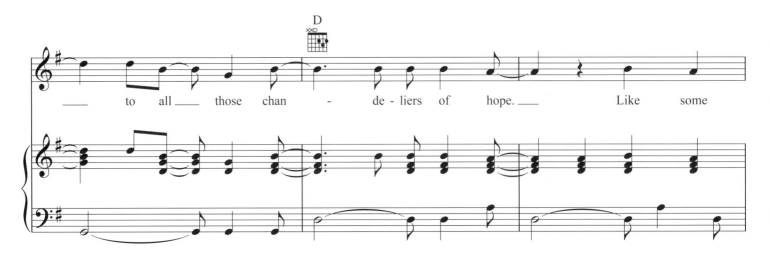

___ to all ___ those chan - de - liers of hope. ___ Like some

drunk - ard in ___ this cit - y, I ___ go sing - ing out of tune, ___

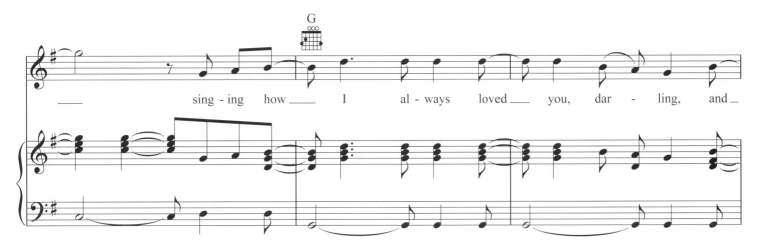

___ sing - ing how ___ I al - ways loved ___ you, dar - ling, and ___

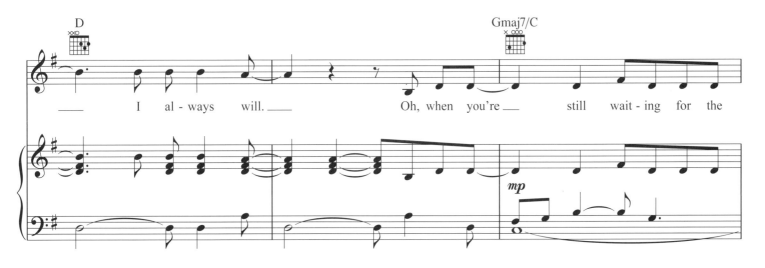

___ I al - ways will. ___ Oh, when you're ___ still wait - ing for the

snow to fall, ___ it does - n't real - ly feel ___ like Christ - mas at all. ___

Still wait-ing for the snow to fall, __ it does-n't real-ly feel __ like Christ-mas at all. __

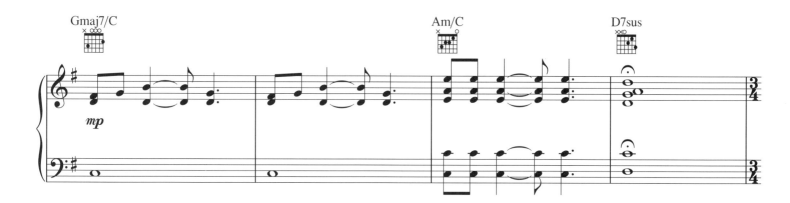

A little slower, with a lilt

Those Christ-mas lights light up the street,
lights light up the street,
lights, light up the street,

down where the sea and cit - y meet.
may - be they'll bring her back to me.
light up the fi - re - works in me.

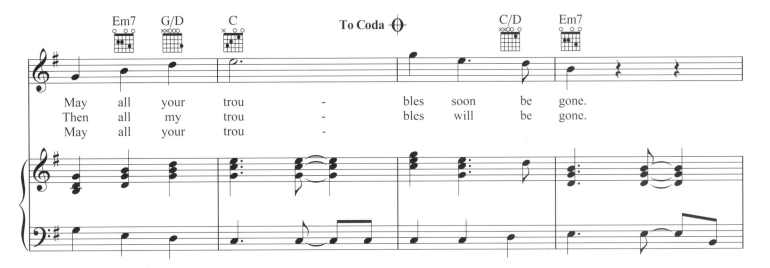

To Coda ⊕

May all your trou - bles soon be gone.
Then all my trou - bles will be gone.
May all your trou -

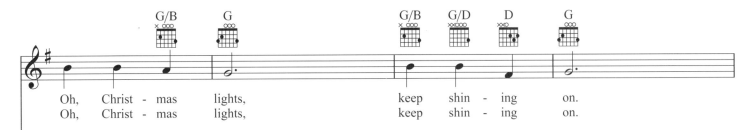

Oh, Christ - mas lights, keep shin - ing on.
Oh, Christ - mas lights, keep shin - ing on.

1
D7sus

Those Christ - mas

2
G/D   D   G

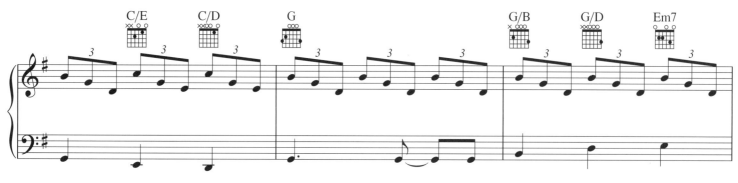

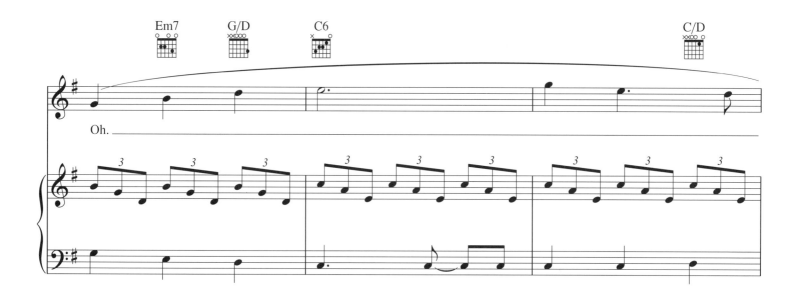

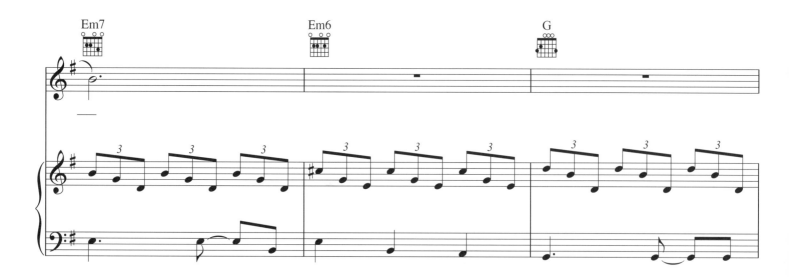

D.S. al Coda

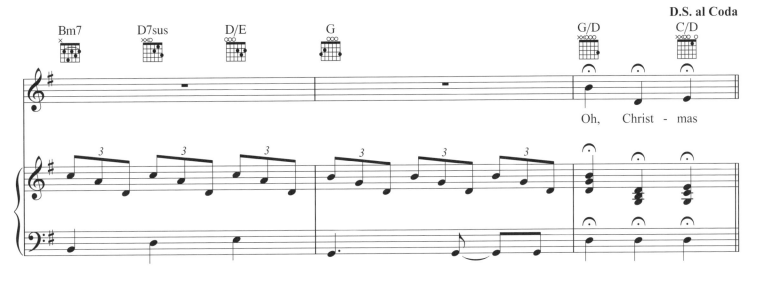

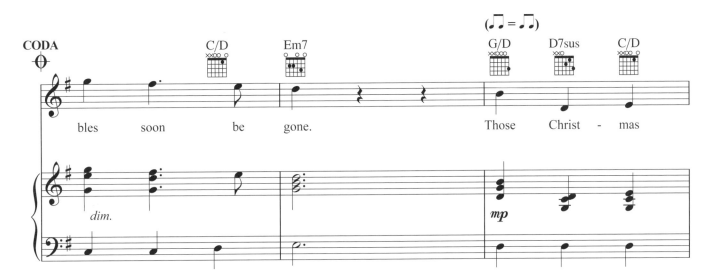

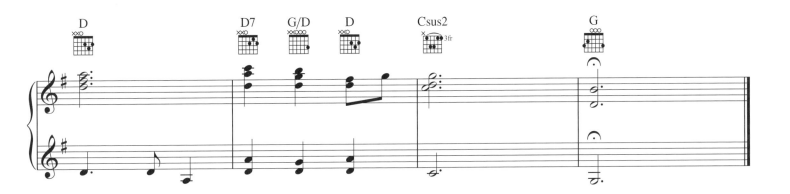

CHRISTMAS SAVES THE YEAR

Words and Music by
TYLER JOSEPH

Snow falls down from the gray ___ sky. Ash - es fall in the sea. ___
Dust off old pho - to box - es. This one's marked nine - ty - two. ___

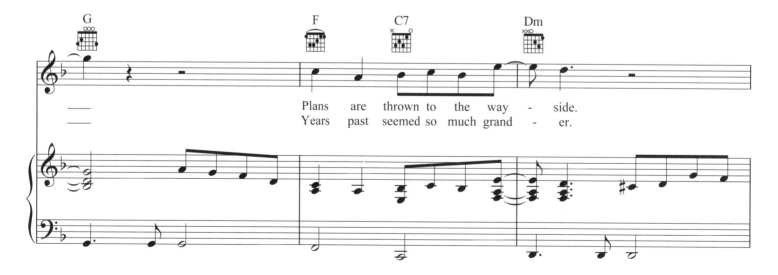

___ Plans are thrown to the way - side.
___ Years past seemed so much grand - er.

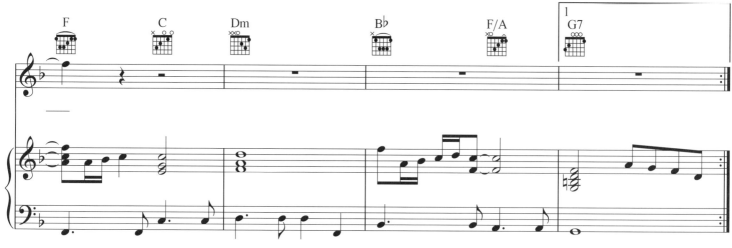

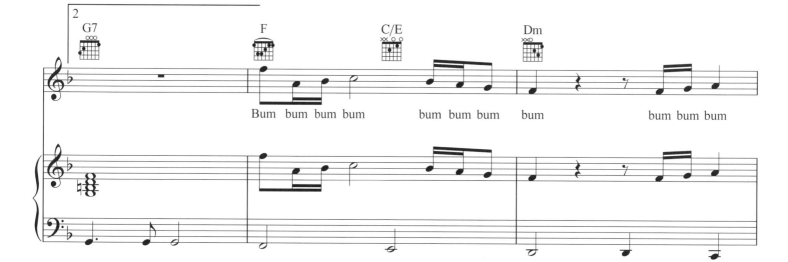

Bum bum bum bum   bum bum bum   bum   bum bum bum

bum   bum bum bum bum   bum _____ bum bum bum.   Ev - 'ry - bod - y

rest as - sured, _ ev - 'ry - bod - y   wants   to _____ make   it _____ home _

this year, e - ven if the world is crum-blin' down. _____ 'Cause ev - 'ry - bod - y's

got some - bod - y who's got their name ____ on a shelf with

cheap dé - cor ____ and fla-vored cheer. ___ You rest as - sured, ___ Christ - mas saves ___ the year. ___

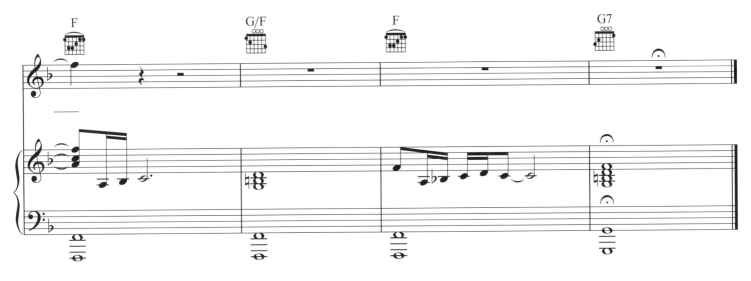

CHRISTMAS TREE FARM

Words and Music by
TAYLOR SWIFT

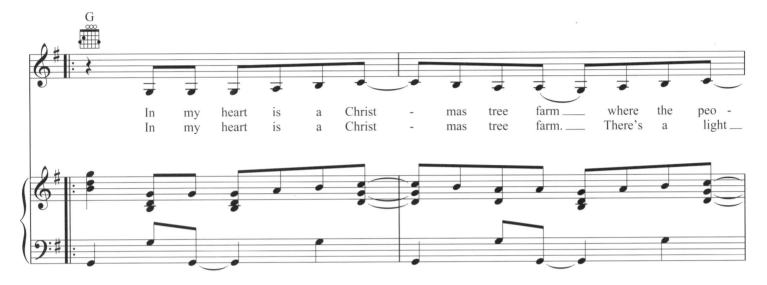

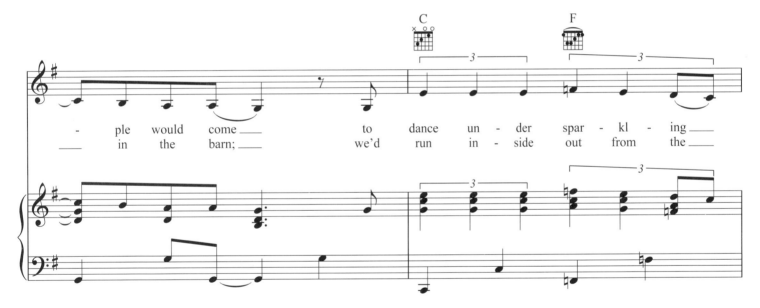

-der would flow. ___ And I just wan - na be there to -
___ and they're safe. ___ They wake to see a blan - ket of ___

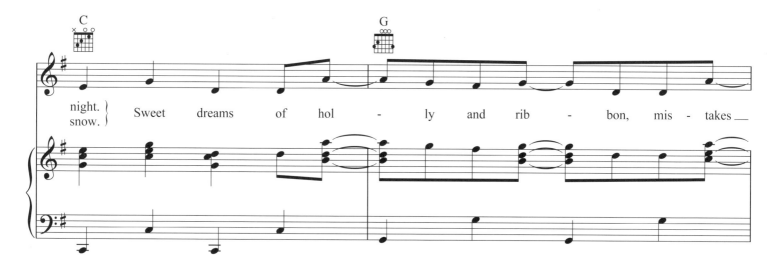

night. } Sweet dreams of hol - ly and rib - bon, mis - takes ___
snow. }

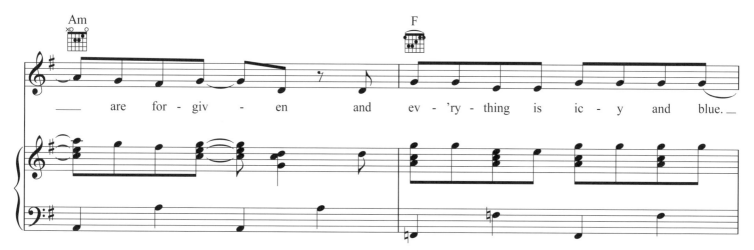

___ are for - giv - en and ev - 'ry - thing is ic - y and blue. ___

And you would be there, ___ too. ___

Un - der the mis - tle - toe, ___

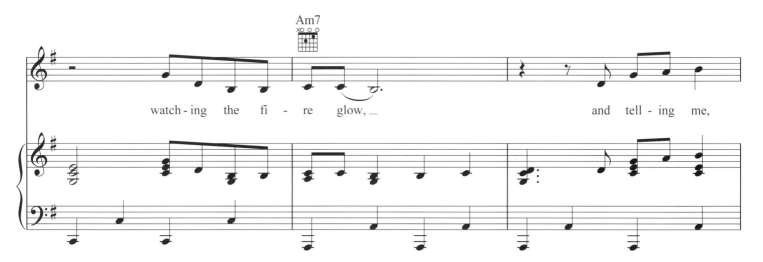

watch - ing the fi - re glow, ___ and tell - ing me,

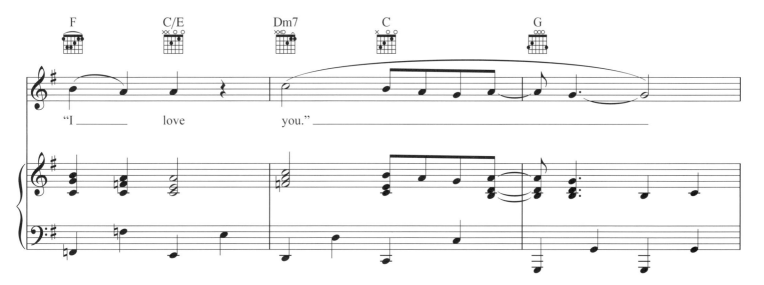

"I ___ love you." _____

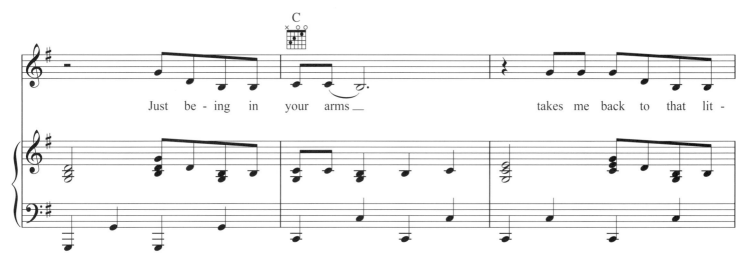

Just be - ing in your arms ___ takes me back to that lit -

tle farm ___ where ev-'ry wish ___ comes

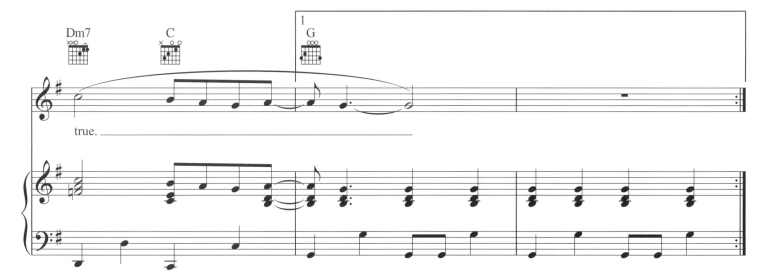

true. ___

___ Ba - by, yeah. ___ And when I'm feel-ing a - lone,

you re-mind me of home. Oh, ba - by, ba - by, mer - ry Christ - mas.

And when the world is-n't fair, I pre-tend that we're there. Ba-by, ba-by, mer-

-ry Christ-mas to you. ____

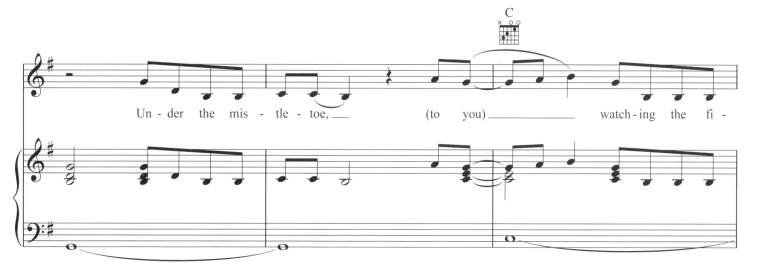

Un-der the mis-tle-toe, ___ (to you) _____ watch-ing the fi-

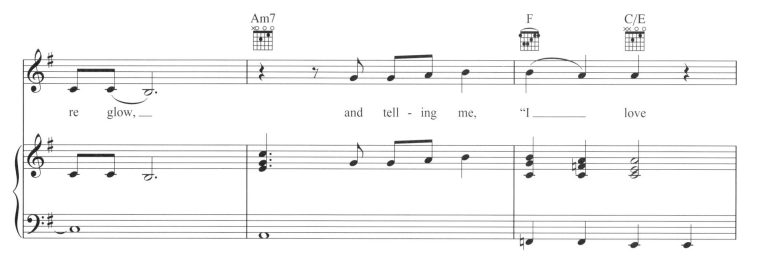

re glow, ___ and tell-ing me, "I _____ love

you." _____ Ba - by, ba - by, mer - ry Christ - mas.

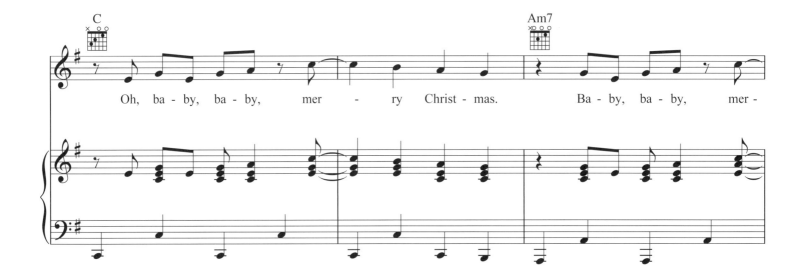

Oh, ba - by, ba - by, mer - ry Christ - mas. Ba - by, ba - by, mer -

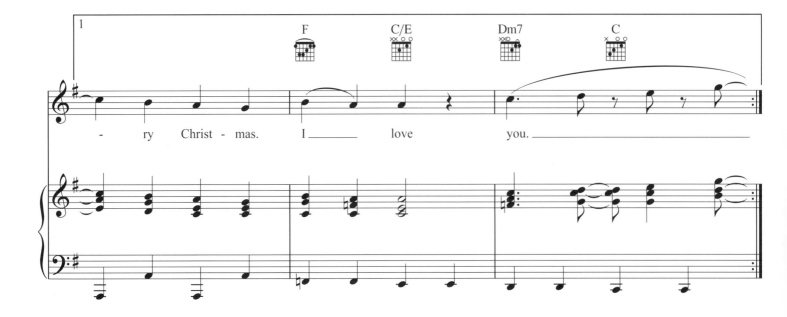

- ry Christ - mas. I _____ love you. _____

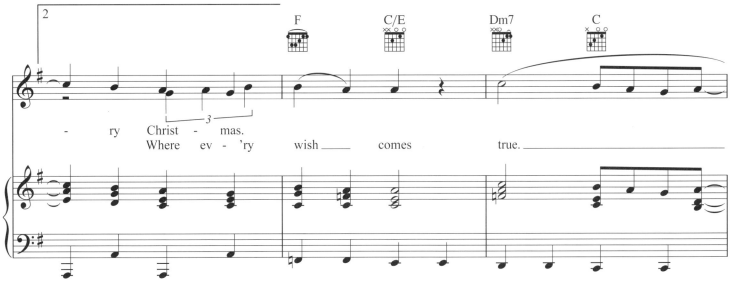

-ry Christ - mas.
Where ev - 'ry wish _____ comes true. _____

(Ooh. _____

Ooh. _____

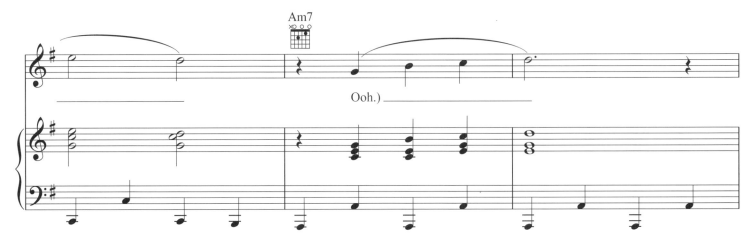

Ooh.) _____

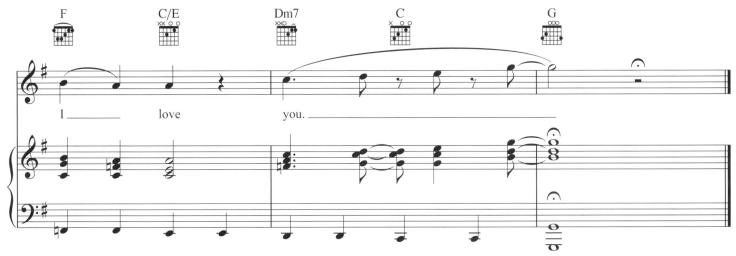

I _____ love you. _____

EVERYDAY IS CHRISTMAS

Words and Music by SIA FURLER
and GREG KURSTIN

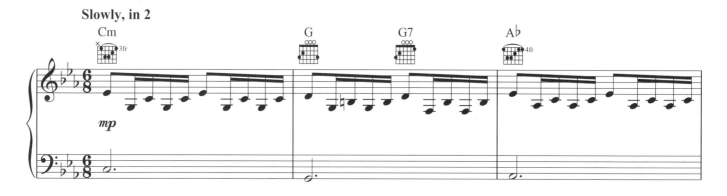

Oh,   Fa - ther Time, _   you and
Oh,   you're my love, _   you're the

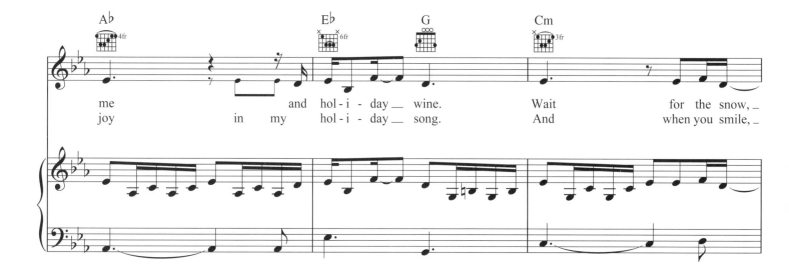

me   and hol - i - day _ wine.   Wait   for the snow, _
joy   in my hol - i - day _ song.   And   when you smile, _

I will read the list that I wrote.)
I can't breathe, can't be-lieve __ that you're mine.)

Sit-ting by the o-pen fi-re, lov-ing you's a gift to-night. Lov-ing you for all my life,

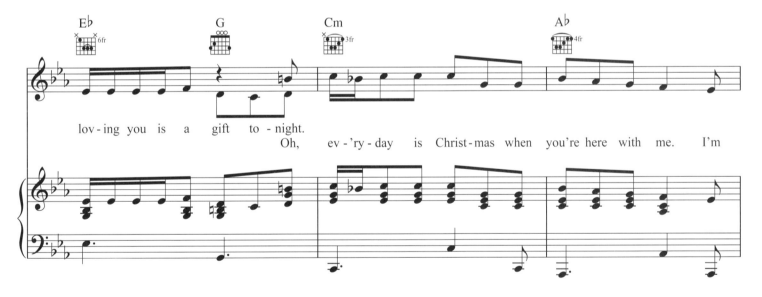

lov-ing you is a gift to-night.
Oh, ev-'ry-day is Christ-mas when you're here with me. I'm

safe in your arms, you're my an-gel, ba-by. Ev-'ry-day is Christ-mas when

you're by my side. You're the gift that keeps giv-ing, my an-gel for life. __

Ev-'ry-day is Christ-mas, ev-'ry-day is Christ-mas, ev-'ry-day is Christ-mas with

you by my side. ___ Ev-'ry-day is Christ-mas, ev-'ry-day is Christ-mas,

ev-'ry-day is Christ-mas with you by my side. ___ you by my side. ___

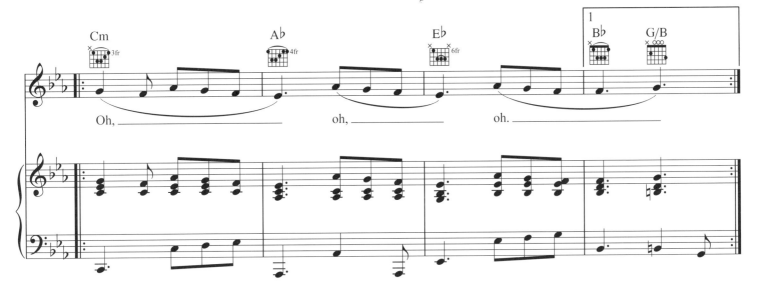

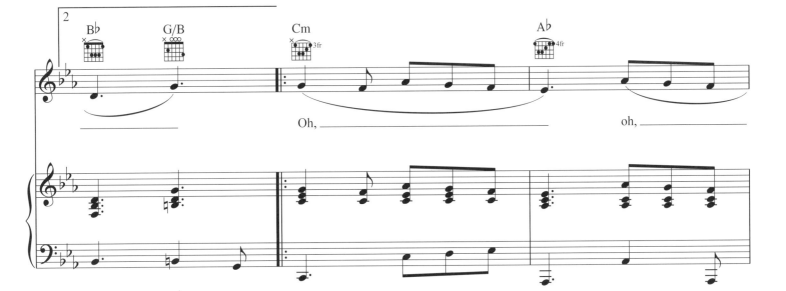

FOR LOVE ON CHRISTMAS DAY

Words and Music by ERIC CLAPTON,
SIMON CLIMIE and DENNIS MORGAN

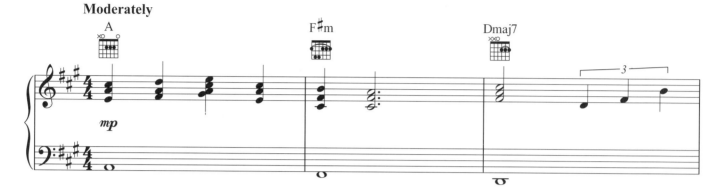

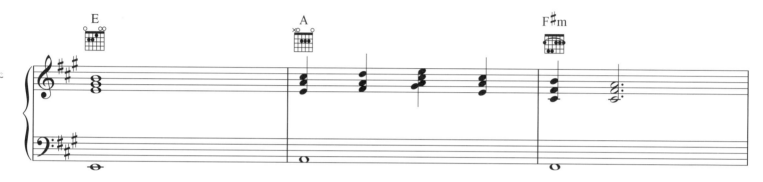

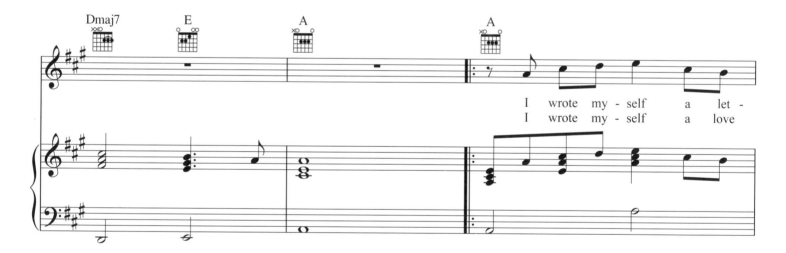

I wrote my-self a let-
I wrote my-self a love

ter.
song

I told my-self a lie
be-liev-in' ev-'ry word,

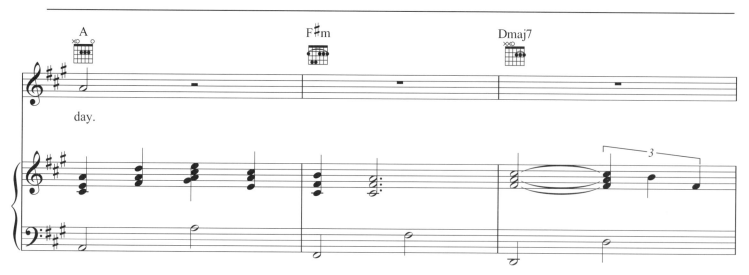

day.

dream world — and dy - ing

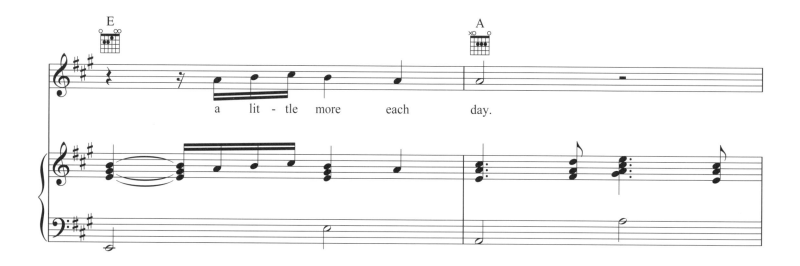

a lit - tle more each day.

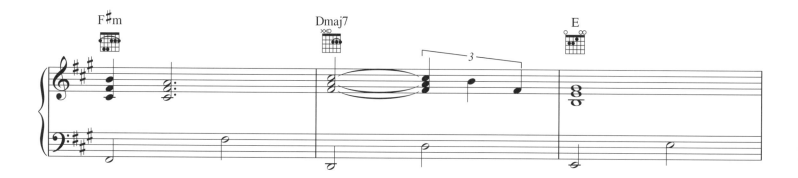

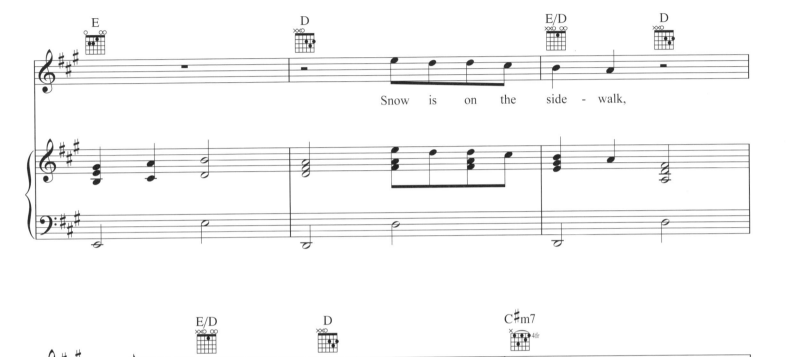

Snow is on the side-walk,

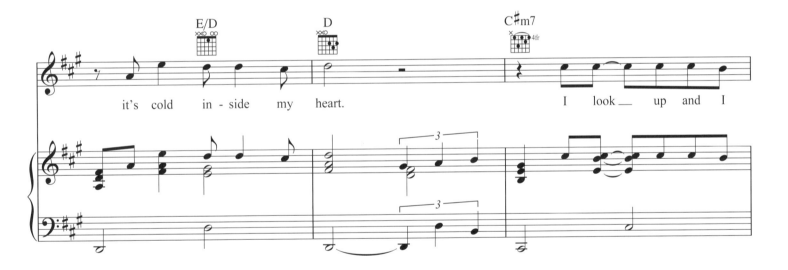

it's cold in-side my heart. I look ___ up and I

won - der have I lost my guid - ing star?

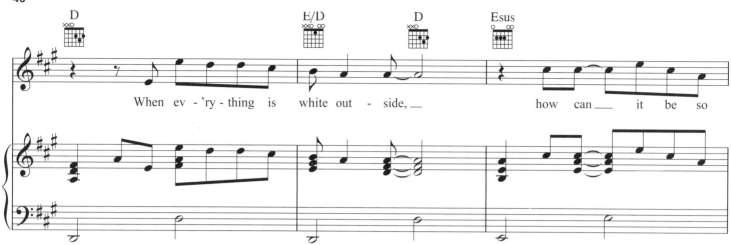

When ev - 'ry - thing is white out - side, __ how can __ it be so

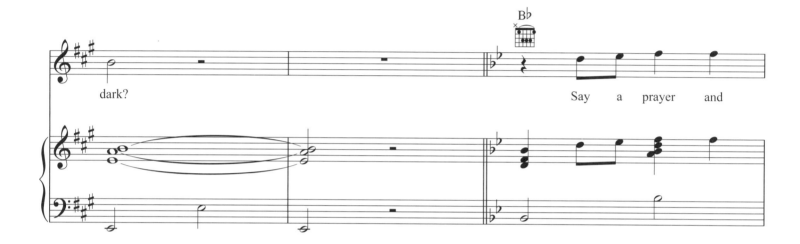

dark? Say a prayer and

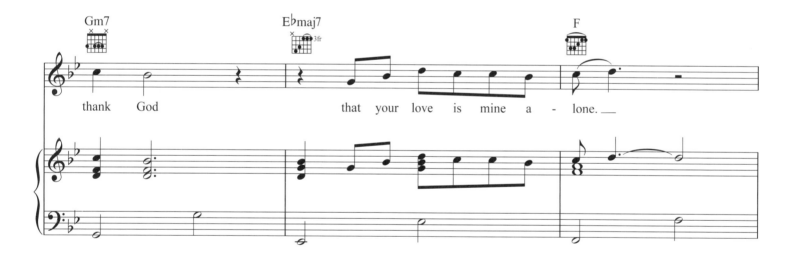

thank God that your love is mine a - lone. __

There'll nev - er be an - oth - er

who could grace our hap-py home. ___ Pray on Christ-mas

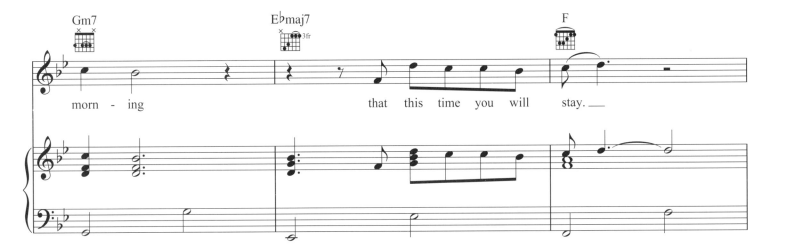

morn - ing that this time you will stay. ___

But I'm liv - in' in a dream world and dy - ing ___

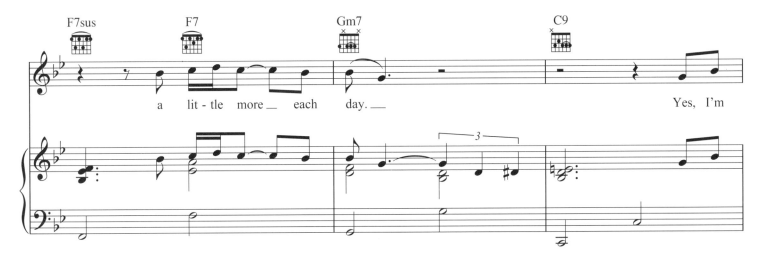

a lit - tle more ___ each day. ___ Yes, I'm

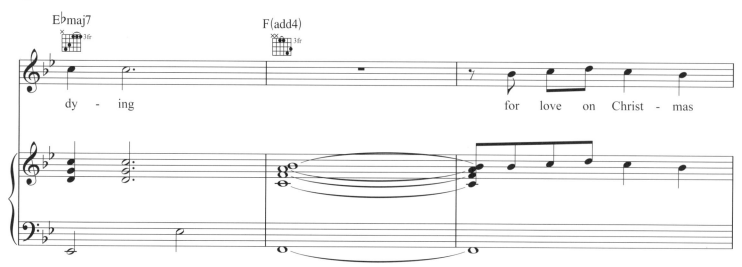

dy - ing

for love on Christ - mas

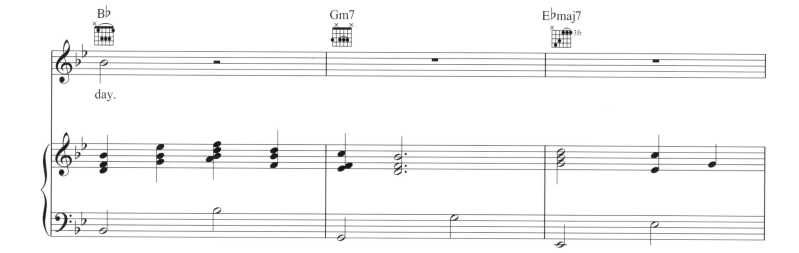

day.

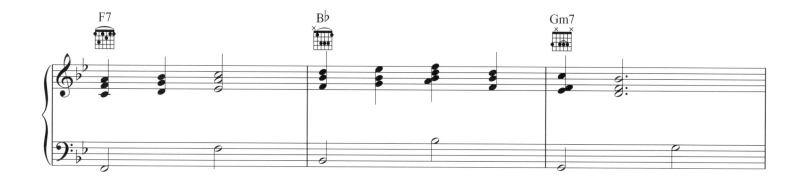

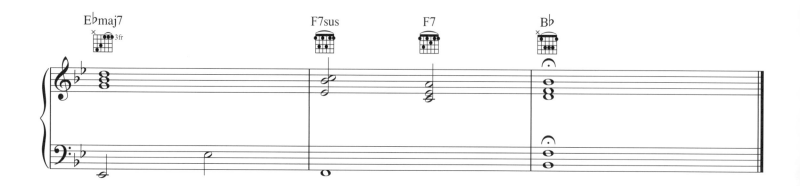

LIGHT OF THE WORLD

Words and Music by LAUREN DAIGLE,
PAUL MABURY and PAUL DUNCAN

Power Ballad

The world waits for a mir-a-cle, ___

the heart waits for a lit-tle bit of hope. O come, ___ O ___ come, ___

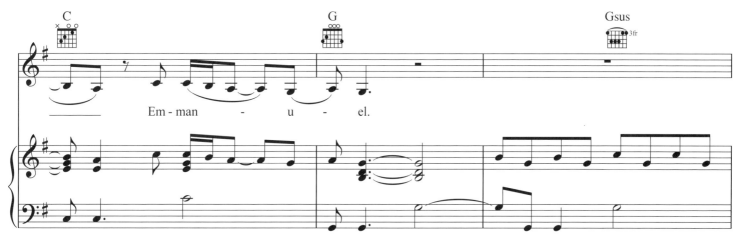

Em-man-u-el.

* *Recorded a half step lower.*

A child prays for peace on __ earth, __ and she's call - ing out __ from a sea __

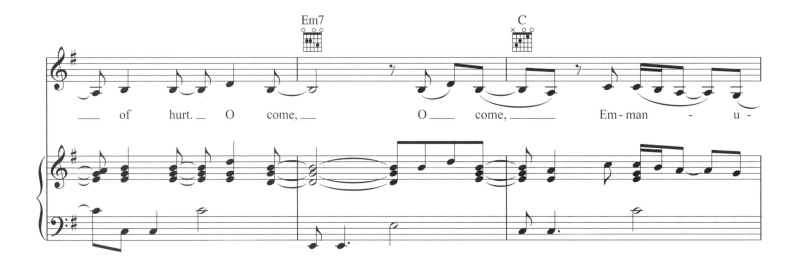

__ of hurt. __ O come, __ O __ come, _____ Em - man - u -

- el. _____ And can you hear the

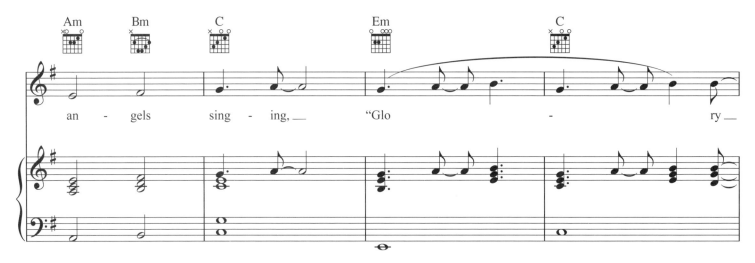

an - gels sing - ing, __ "Glo - ry __

to the Light of the world"? __ Glo -

- ry, _____ the Light of the world ___ is _____

here. The drought breaks with the tears of a moth - er.

A ba-by's cry is the sound of love __ come down, __ come _ down, _

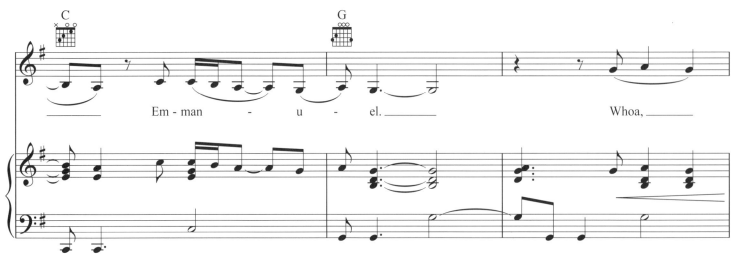

Em - man - u - el. _____ Whoa, _____

He is the song for the suf - fer - ing. ___ He is Mes - si - ah; the

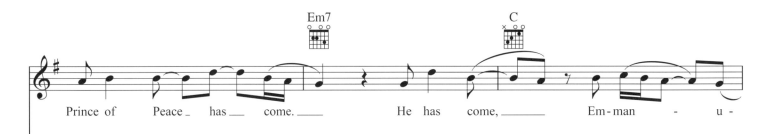

Prince of Peace _ has _ come. ___ He has come, _____ Em - man - u -

- el, _____ oh. _____ Glo - ry _

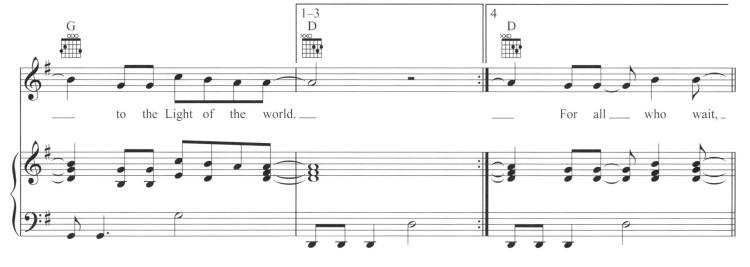

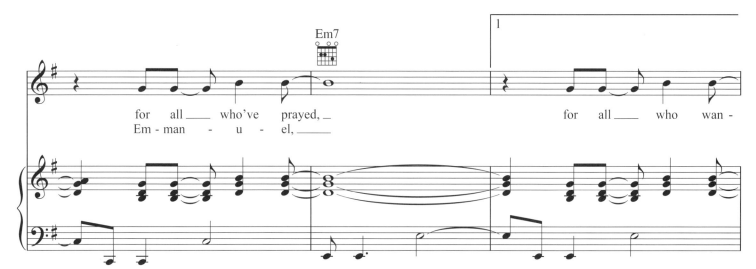

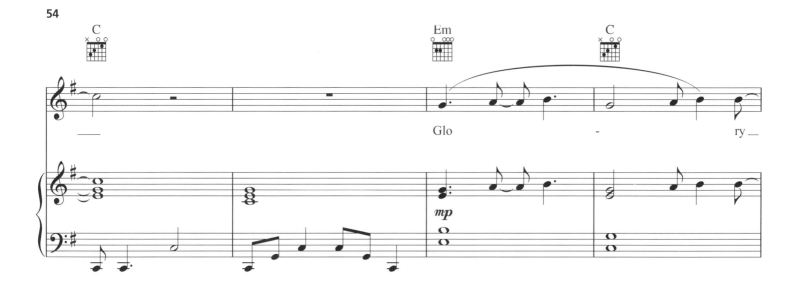

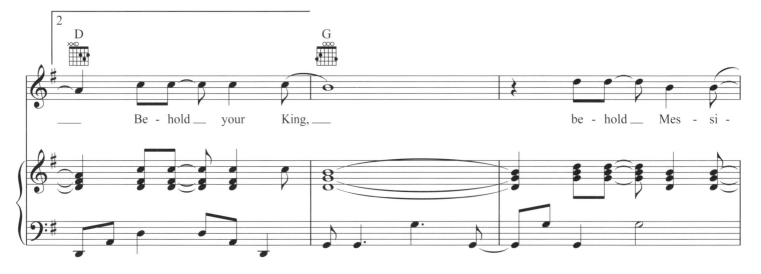

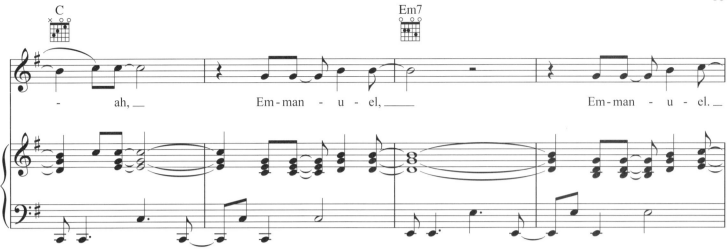

- ah, ___ Em-man-u-el, ___ Em-man-u-el. ___

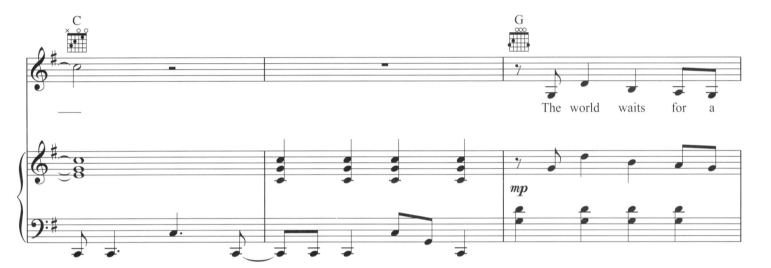

___ The world waits for a

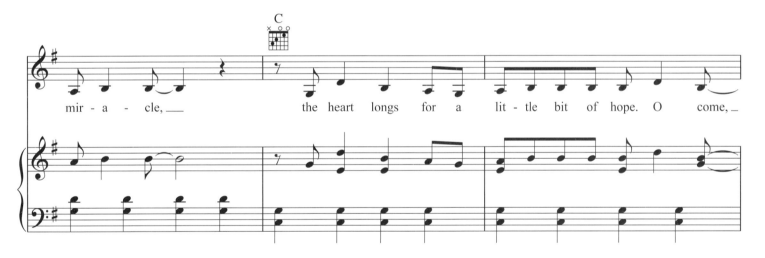

mir-a-cle, ___ the heart longs for a lit-tle bit of hope. O come, ___

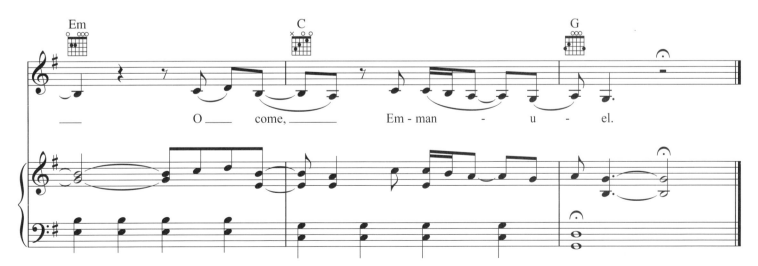

___ O ___ come, ___ Em-man-u-el.

GLITTERY

Words and Music by KACEY MUSGRAVES
and DANIEL TASHIAN

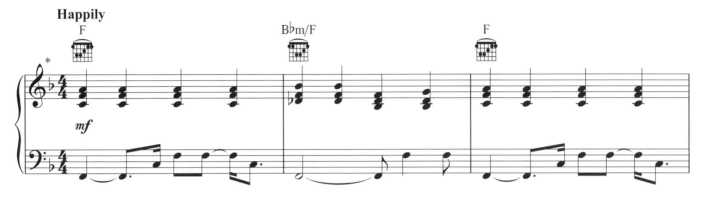

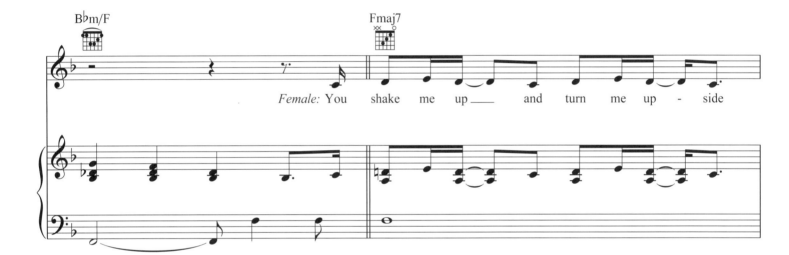

Female: You shake me up ___ and turn me up - side

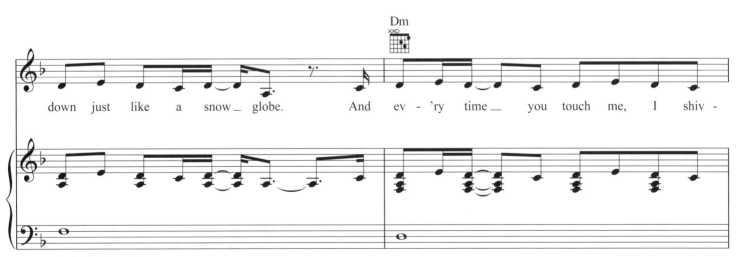

down just like a snow ___ globe. And ev - 'ry time ___ you touch me, I shiv -

* *Recorded a half step lower.*

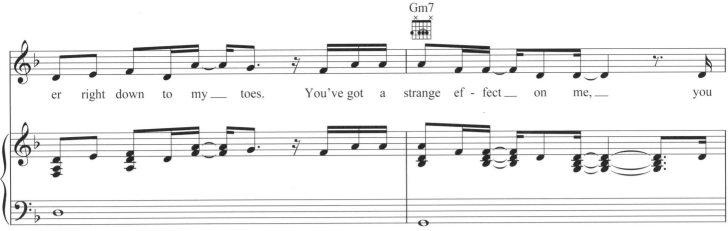

er right down to my ___ toes. You've got a strange ef - fect ___ on me, ___ you

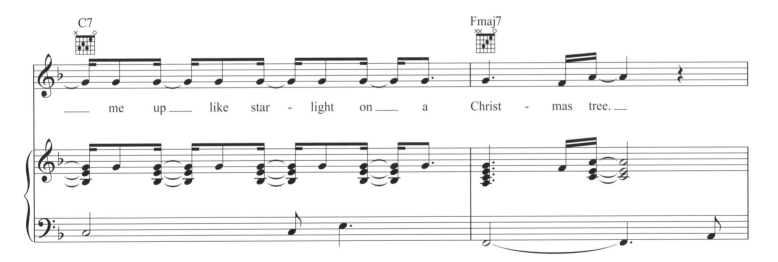

know you make ___ me feel so glit - ter - y. ___ You light ___

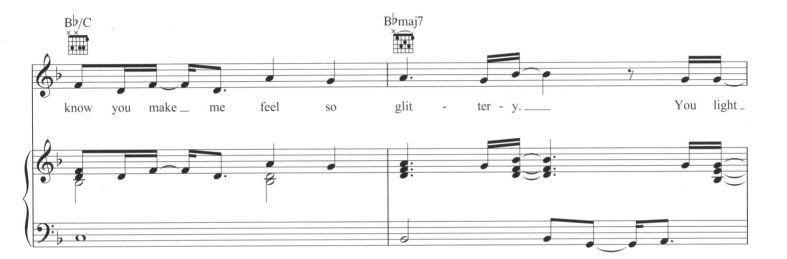

___ me up ___ like star - light on ___ a Christ - mas tree. ___

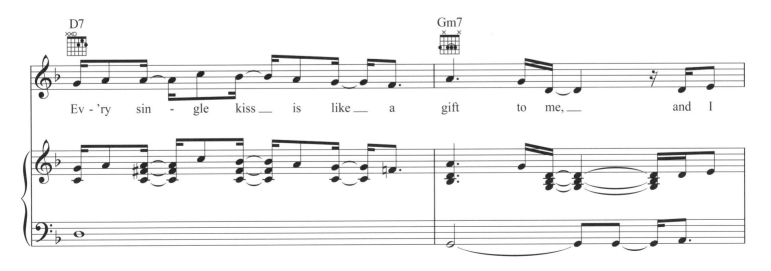

Ev - 'ry sin - gle kiss ___ is like ___ a gift to me, ___ and I

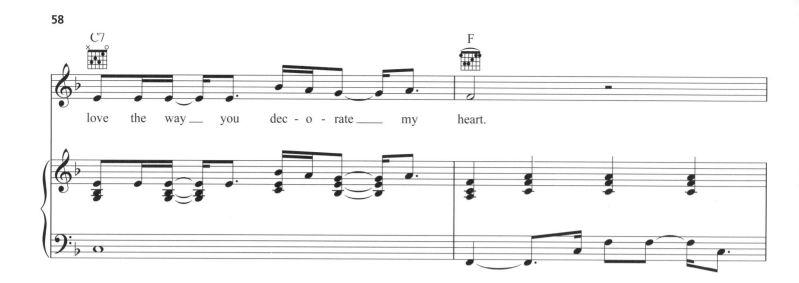

love the way — you dec - o - rate — my heart.

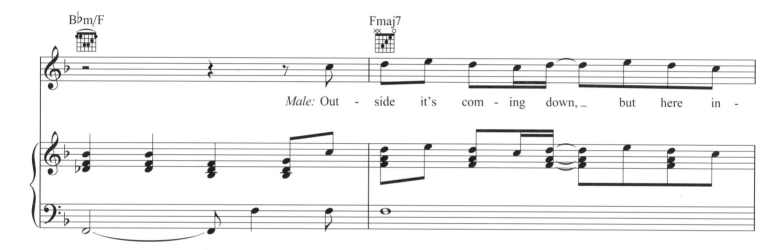

Male: Out - side it's com - ing down, — but here in -

side it's warm - ing up, — so when you take — your time, you turn me

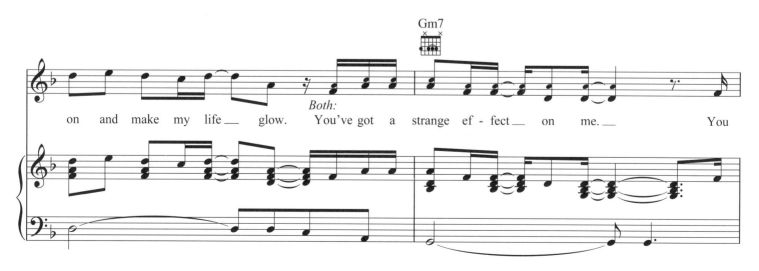

on and make my life — glow. *Both:* You've got a strange ef - fect — on me. — You

make me feel so glit - ter - y. ____ You light ____

____ me up ____ like star - light on ____ a Christ - mas tree. ____

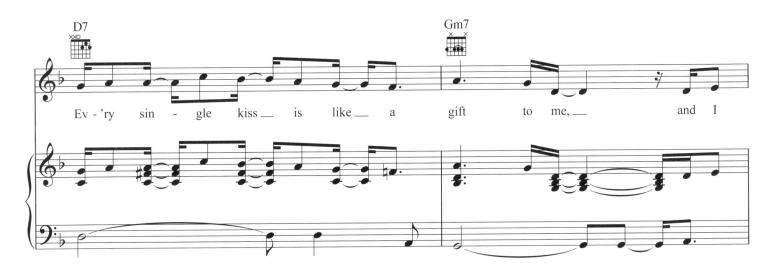

Ev - 'ry sin - gle kiss ____ is like ____ a gift to me, ____ and I

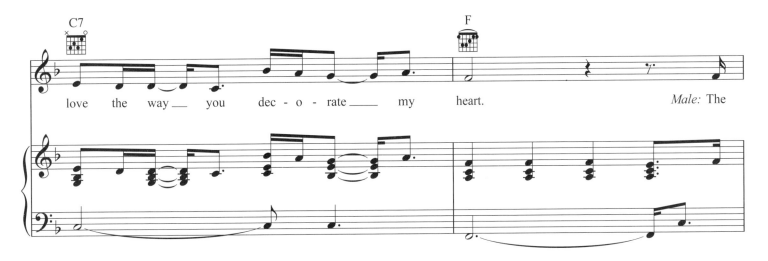

love the way ____ you dec - o - rate ____ my heart.

Male: The

win- ter is___ so gray,___ feels like the ice is here to stay.___ *Female:* But

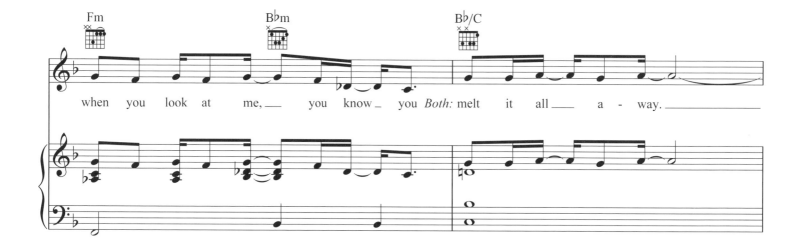

when you look at me,___ you know___ you *Both:* melt it all___ a - way.___

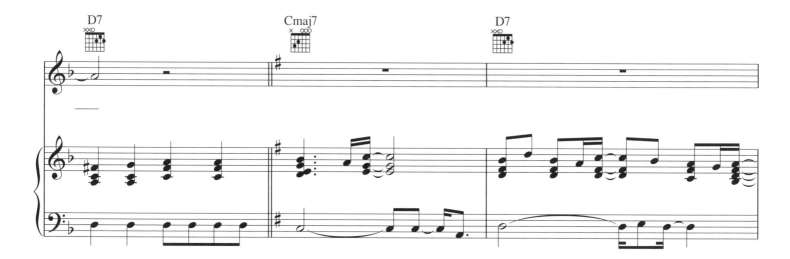

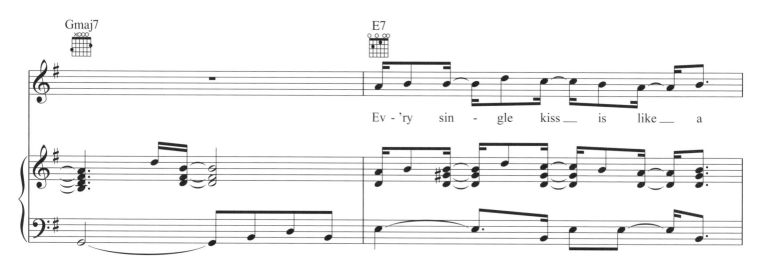

Ev - 'ry sin - gle kiss___ is like___ a

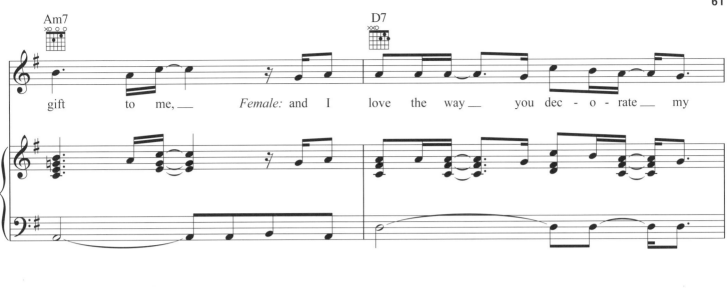

gift to me, ___ *Female:* and I love the way ___ you dec - o - rate ___ my

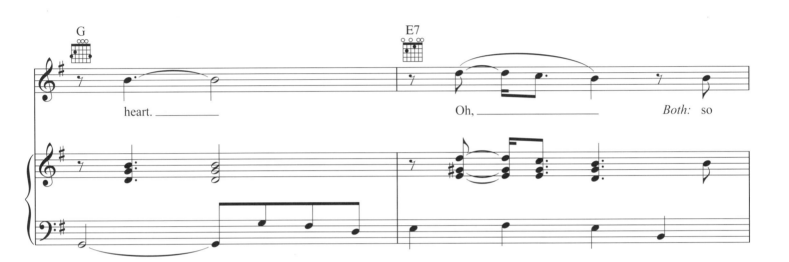

heart. _____ Oh, _____ *Both:* so

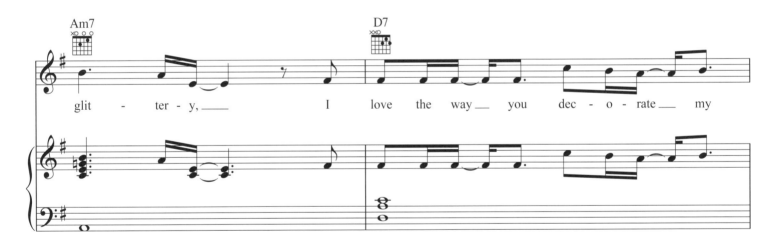

glit - ter - y, ___ I love the way ___ you dec - o - rate ___ my

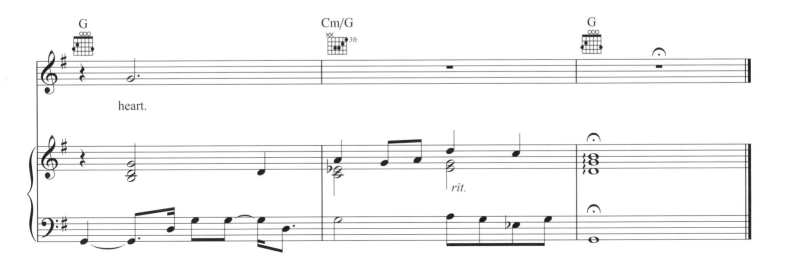

heart.

HALLELUJAH

Words and Music by JOHN STEPHENS
and TOBY GAD

Slowly, in 2

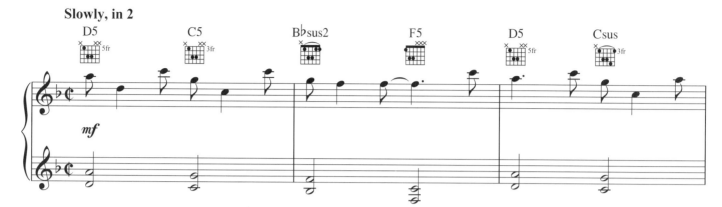

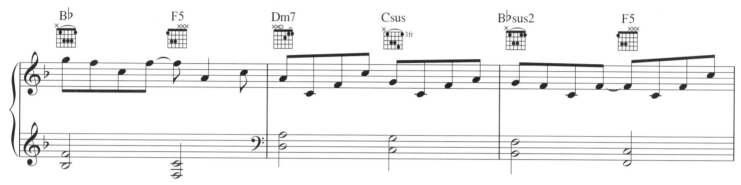

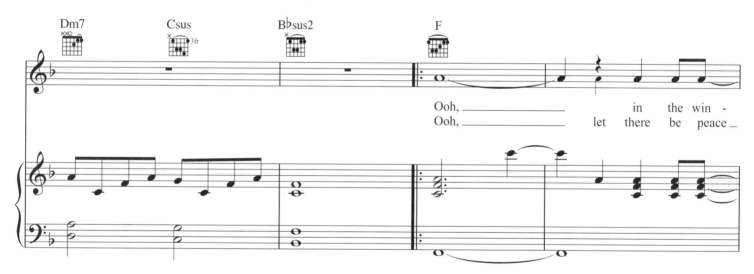

Ooh, _____ in the win -
Ooh, _____ let there be peace _

-ter's chill, _____ let the can - dles light the night _
___ on earth. _____ Let the lone - ly join to - geth -

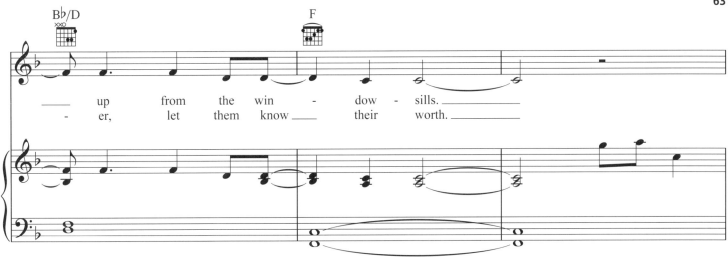

up from the win - dow - sills. _____
- er, let them know _____ their worth. _____

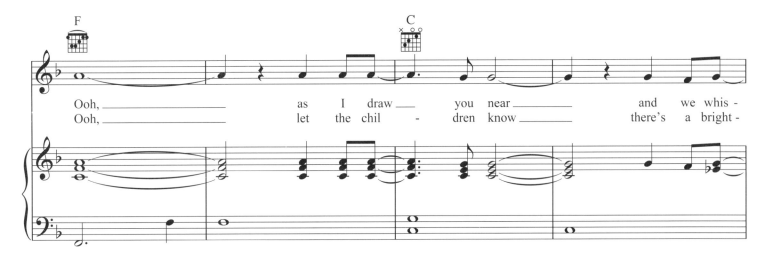

Ooh, _____ as I draw _____ you near _____ and we whis -
Ooh, _____ let the chil - dren know _____ there's a bright -

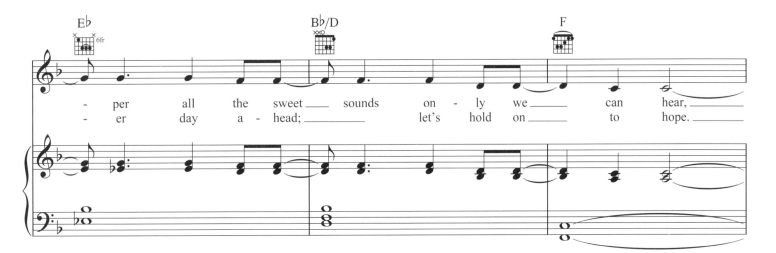

- per all the sweet _____ sounds on - ly we _____ can hear, _____
- er day a - head; _____ let's hold on _____ to hope. _____

_____ on the cold - est eve - ning in this De -
And on the cold - est eve - ning in this De -

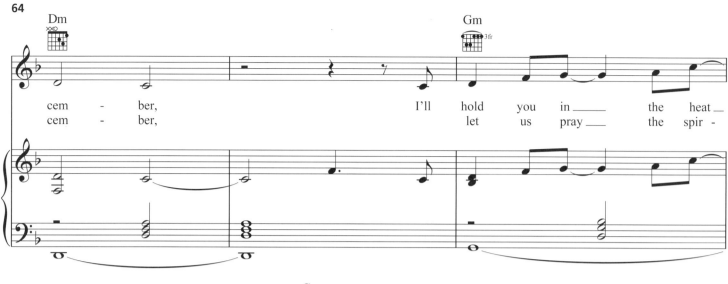

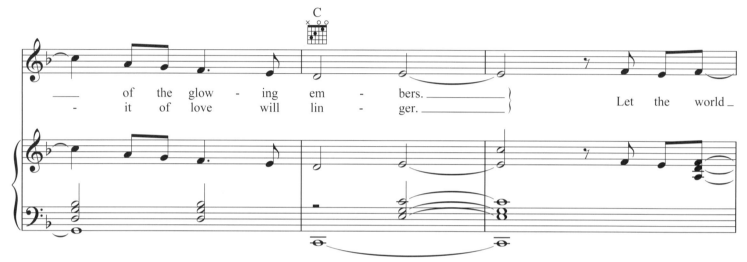

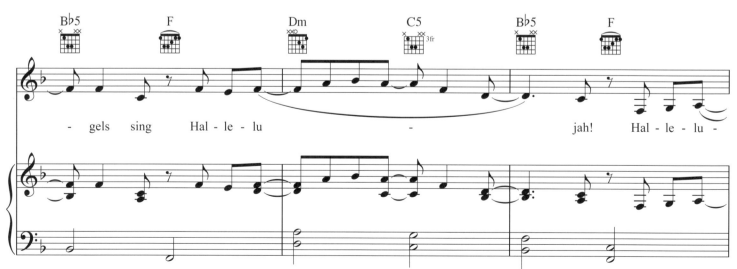

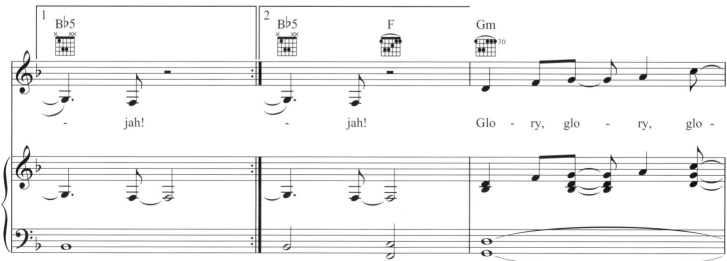

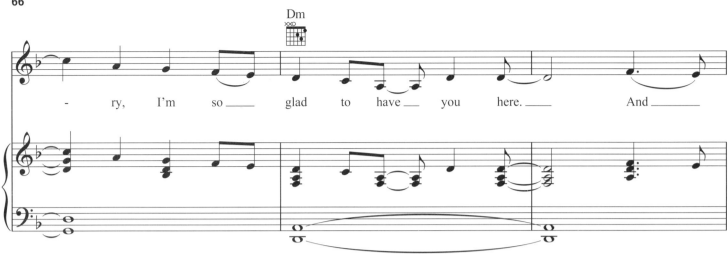

-ry, I'm so ___ glad to have ___ you here. ___ And ___

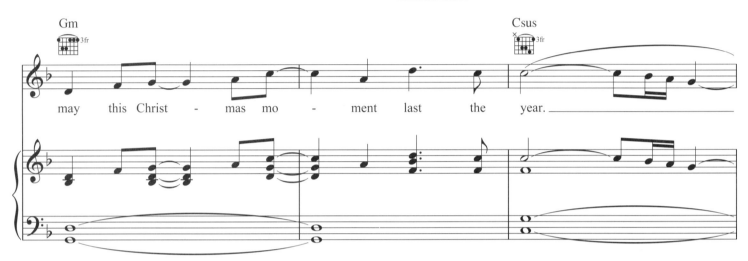

may this Christ - mas mo - ment last the year. ___

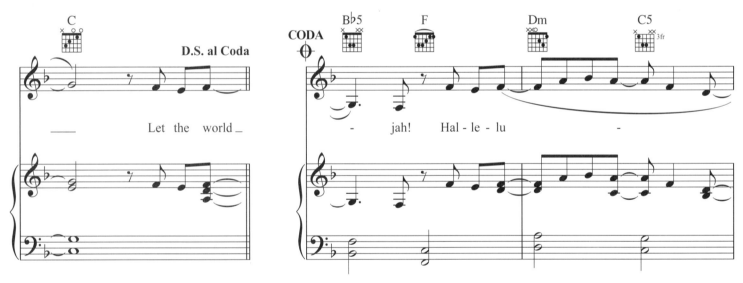

D.S. al Coda

Let the world ___

CODA

- jah! Hal - le - lu -

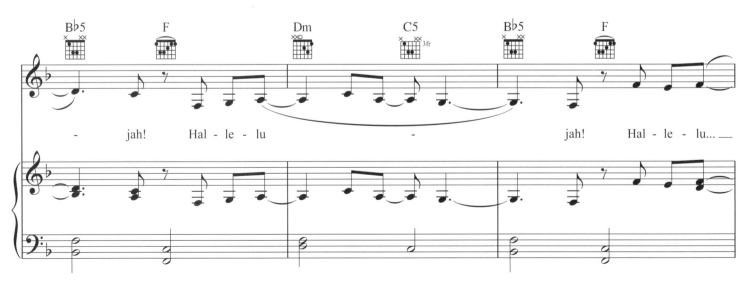

- jah! Hal - le - lu - jah! Hal - le - lu...

HE SHALL REIGN FOREVERMORE

Words and Music by CHRIS TOMLIN
and MATT MAHER

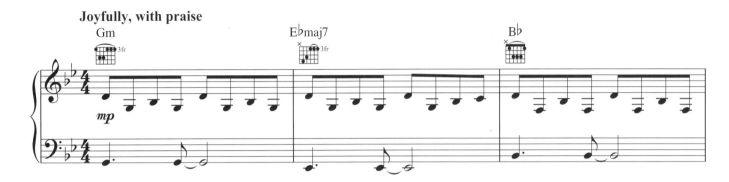

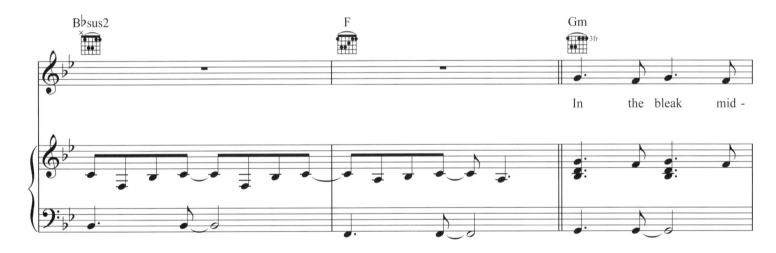

In the bleak mid-

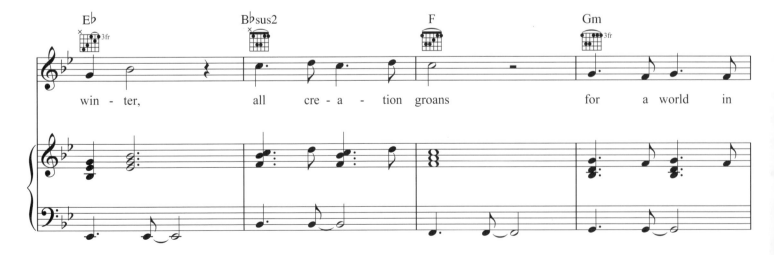

win- ter, all cre-a-tion groans for a world in

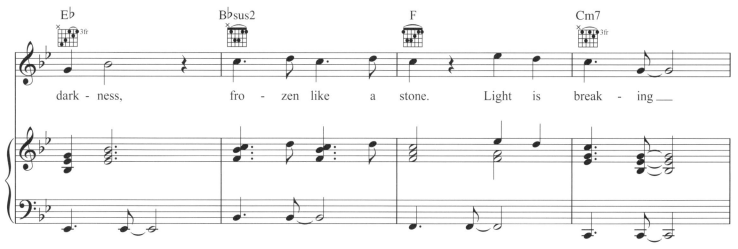

darkness, fro-zen like a stone. Light is break-ing ___

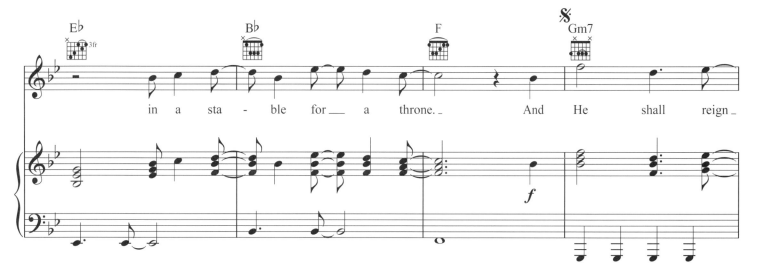

in a sta-ble for ___ a throne. ___ And He shall reign ___

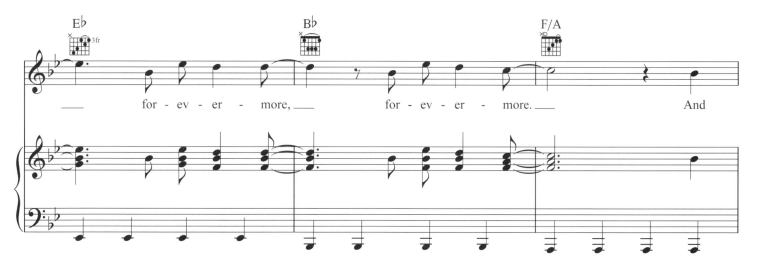

___ for-ev-er-more, ___ for-ev-er-more. ___ And

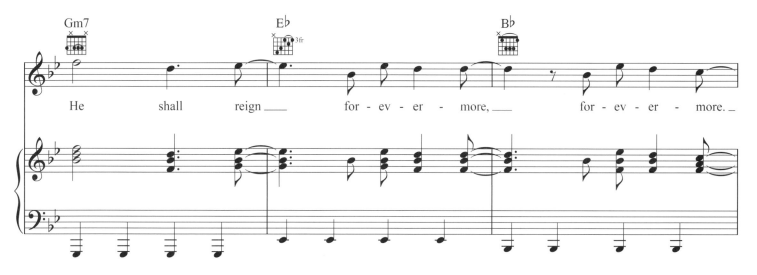

He shall reign ___ for-ev-er-more, ___ for-ev-er-more. ___

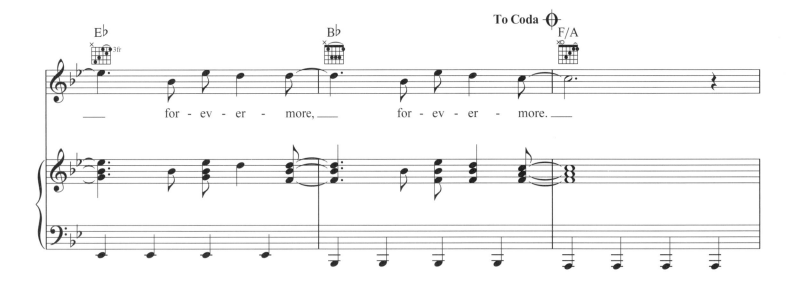

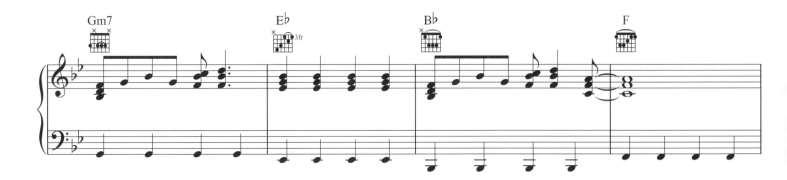

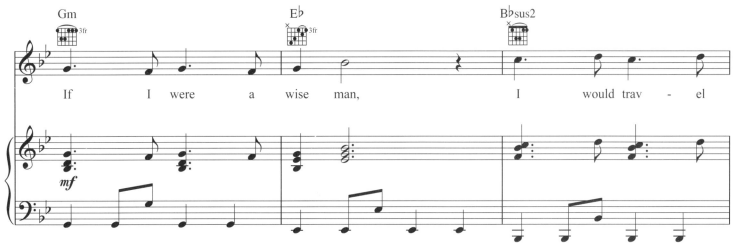

If I were a wise man, I would trav - el far.

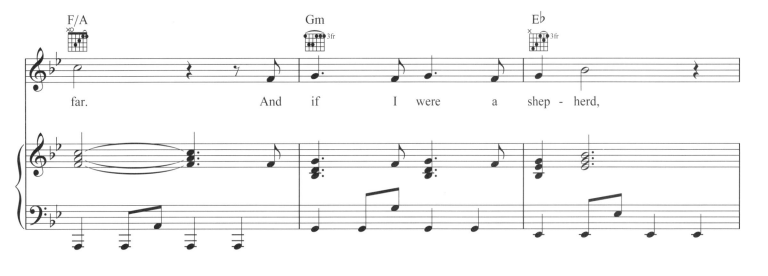

far. And if I were a shep - herd,

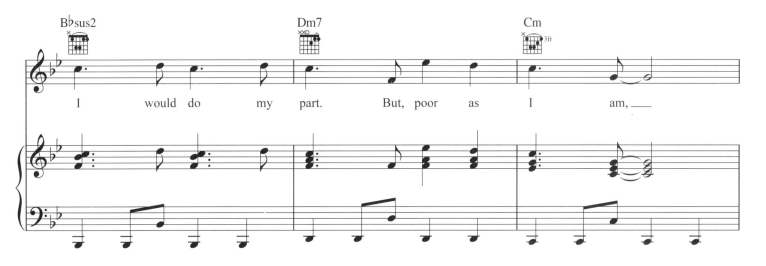

I would do my part. But, poor as I am, ___

I will give ___ to Him ___ my ___ heart. ___ And

D.S. al Coda

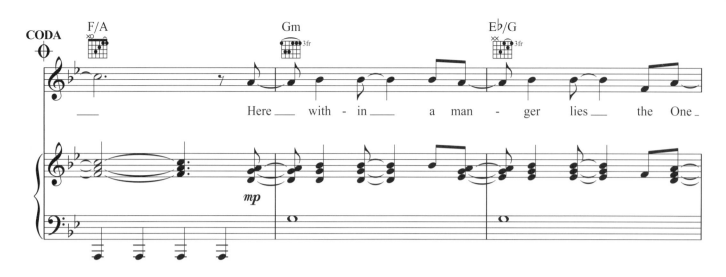

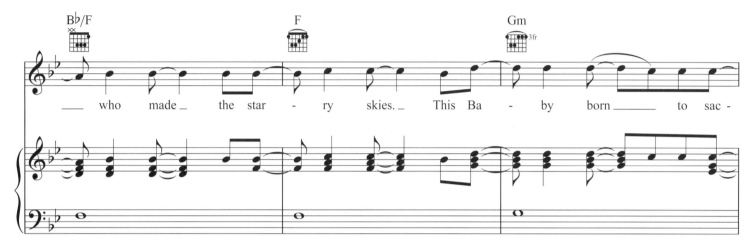

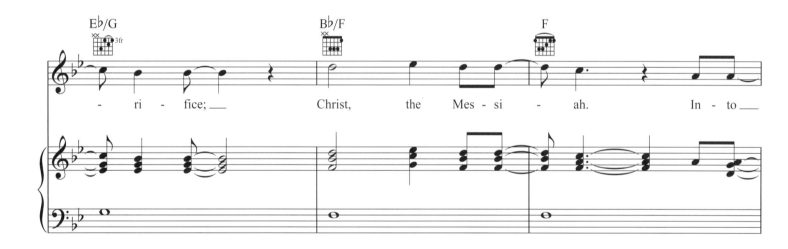

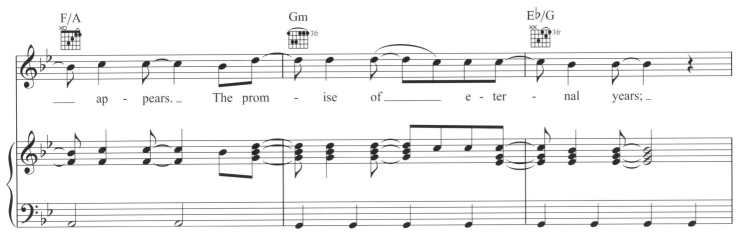

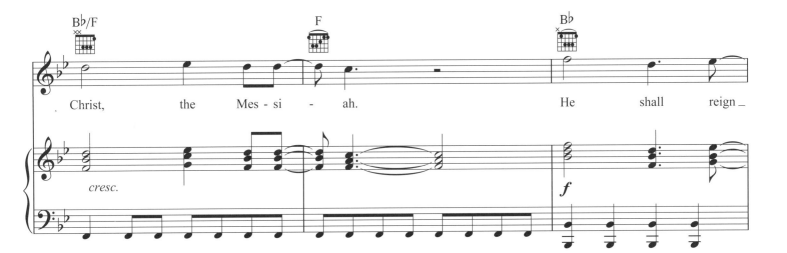

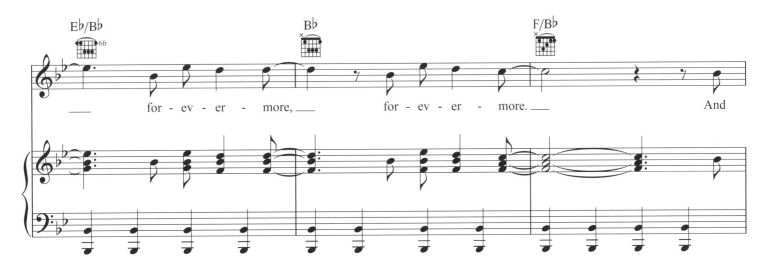

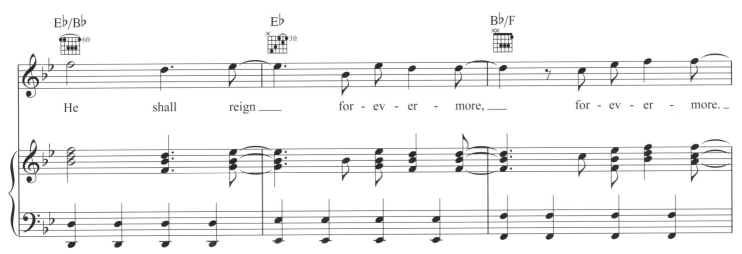

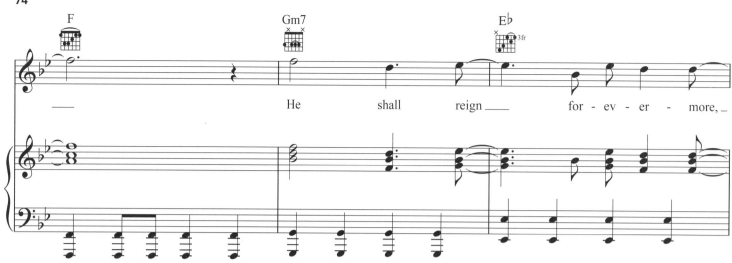

He shall reign _____ for - ev - er - more, _____

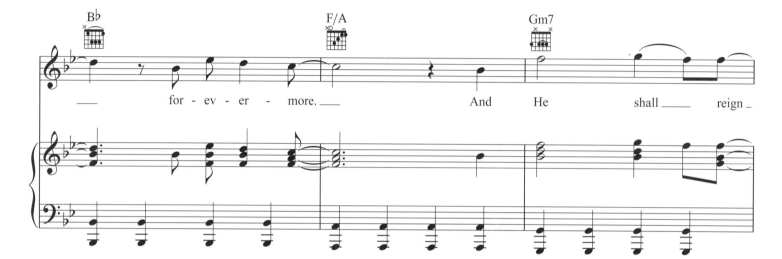

_____ for - ev - er - more. _____ And He shall _____ reign _

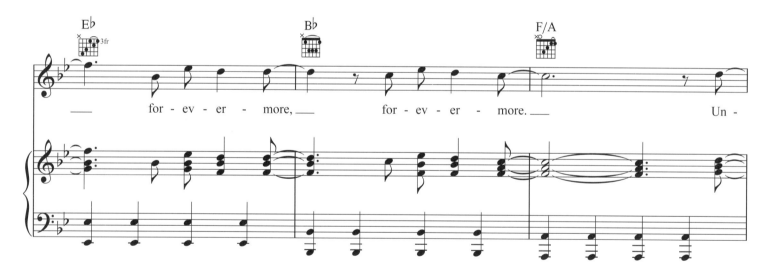

_____ for - ev - er - more, _____ for - ev - er - more. _____ Un -

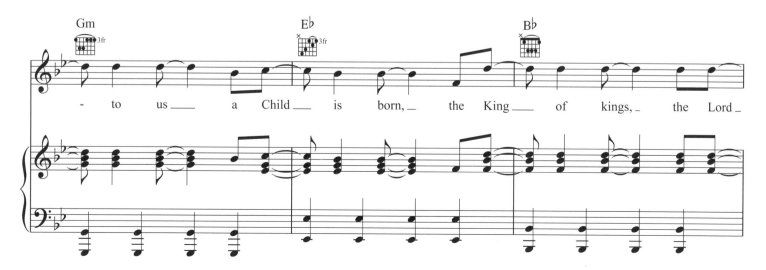

- to us _____ a Child _____ is born, _____ the King _____ of kings, _____ the Lord _

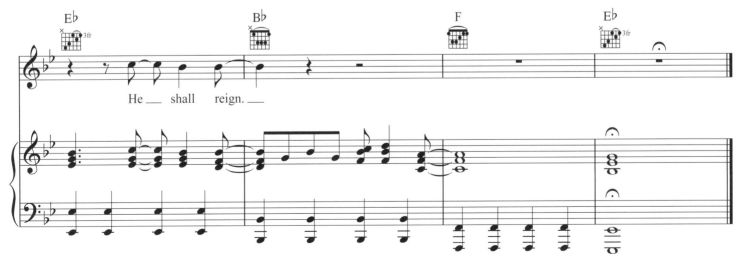

I NEED YOU CHRISTMAS

Words and Music by MARC SIBLEY,
NATHAN CUNNINGHAM, JOEL ESTEVAN CASTILLO,
CONNOR McDONOUGH and RILEY McDONOUGH

Moderately slow

I need you, ___ Christ-mas. ___
I miss the ___ feel-ing, ___

Friends by the fire ___ to hold.
wait-ing for San-ta ___ to show,

Times have been lone — ly, ____ and late — ly I just feel _____ a —
car — ol — ing late night, ____ and all the chil — dren's eyes _____ a —

lone. _____ I need you, __
glow. _____ I need you, __

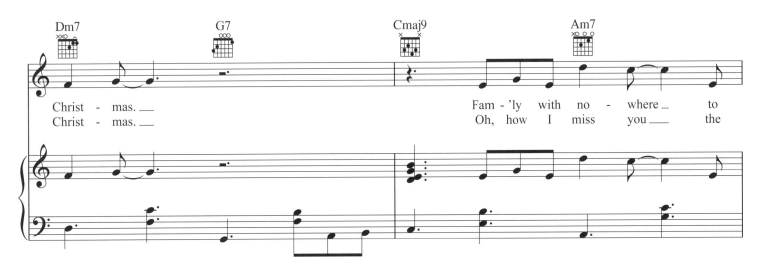

Christ — mas. __ Fam — 'ly with no — where __ to
Christ — mas. __ Oh, how I miss you ____ the

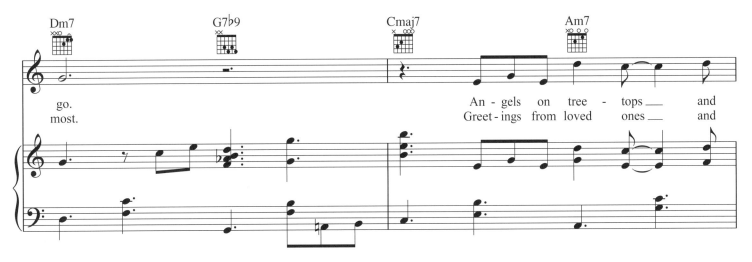

go. An — gels on tree — tops ____ and
most. Greet — ings from loved ones ____ and

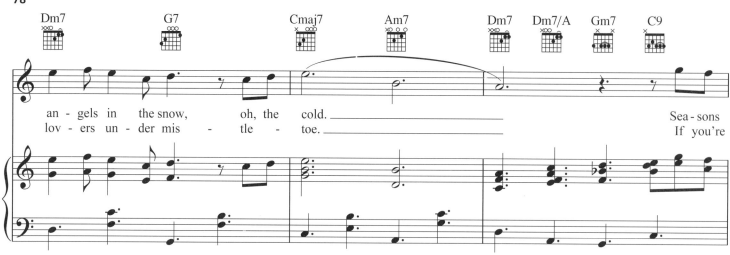

an - gels in the snow, oh, the cold. _____ Sea - sons
lov - ers un - der mis - tle - toe. _____ If you're

change, come and go, but there's one thing I know:
young, if you're old, we all wait to be told

you just ___ stay the same, you don't ___ ev - er change.

just a ___ sim-ple phrase: "Have a mer - ry Christ - mas." _____

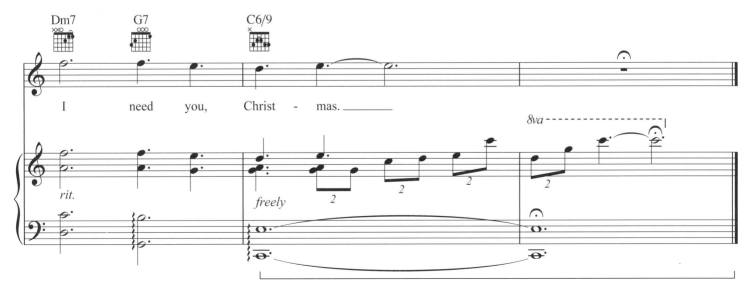

LET THERE BE PEACE

Words and Music by CHRIS DeSTEFANO,
CARRIE UNDERWOOD and BRETT JAMES

Slow Gospel, with freedom

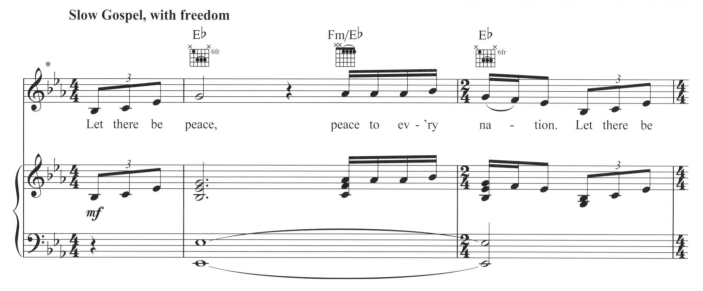

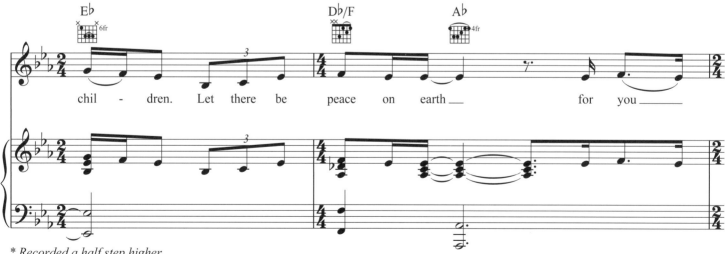

* Recorded a half step higher.

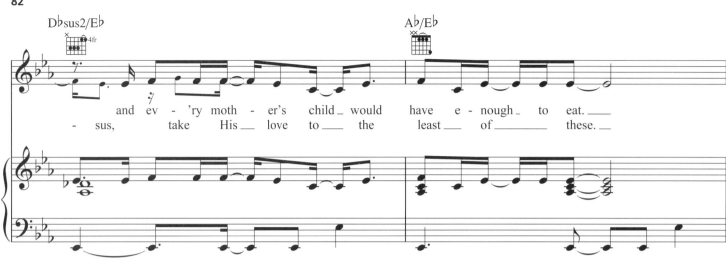

and ev - 'ry moth - er's child __ would have e - nough __ to eat. __
- sus, take His love to __ the least __ of __ these. __

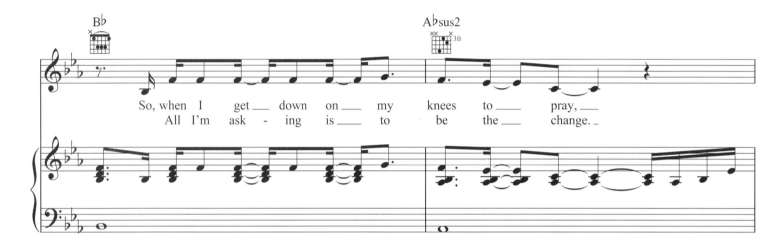

So, when I get __ down on __ my knees to __ pray, __
All I'm ask - ing is __ to be the __ change. __

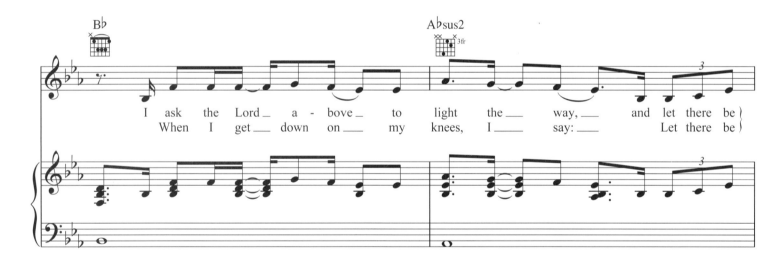

I ask the Lord __ a - bove to light the __ way, __ and let there be
When I get __ down on __ my knees, I __ say: __ Let there be

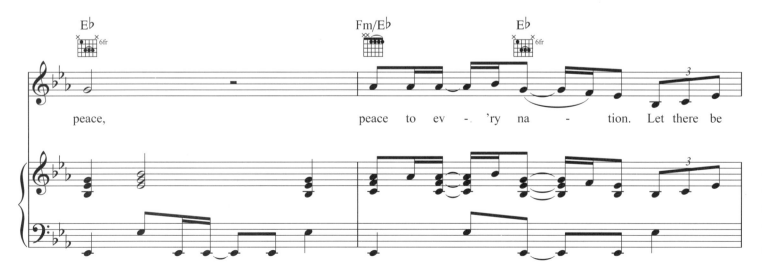

peace, peace to ev - 'ry na - tion. Let there be

hope _____ for all the world to see. ____ And let there be

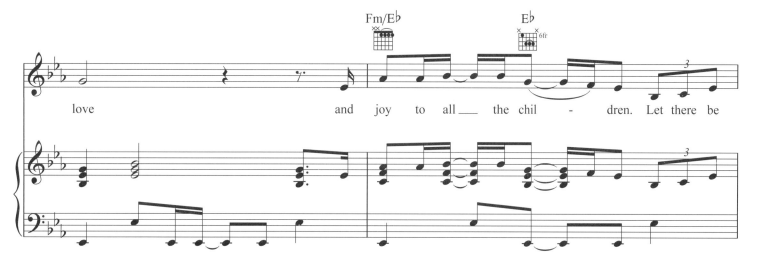

love and joy to all ___ the chil - dren. Let there be

peace on ___ earth _ for you and _ me. ____ you and _ me. ____ Let there be

peace, let there be love, let there be joy for

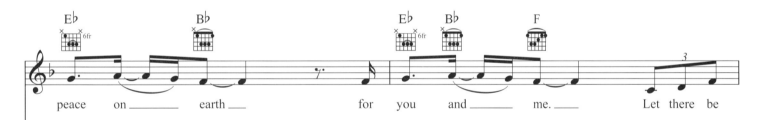

THE LIGHTHOUSE KEEPER

Words and Music by SAM SMITH
and TIMOTHY McKENZIE

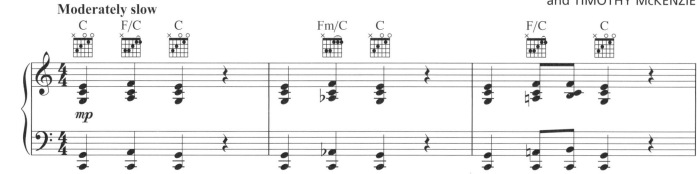

Build your-self a boat, babe, make your-self a sail, float in-to the

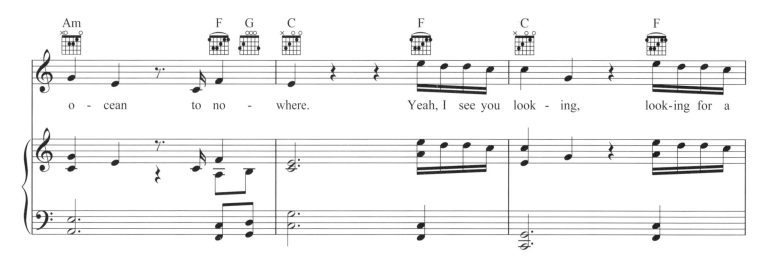

o - cean to no - where. Yeah, I see you look - ing, look-ing for a

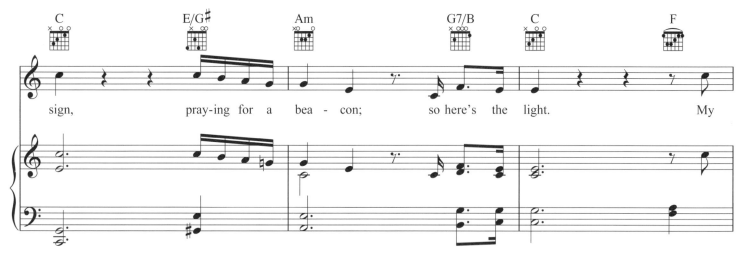

sign, pray-ing for a bea - con; so here's the light. My

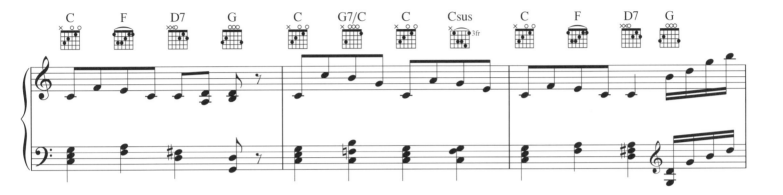

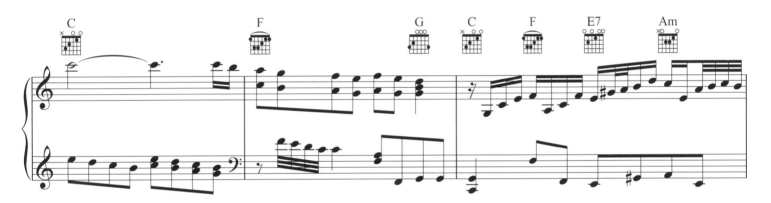

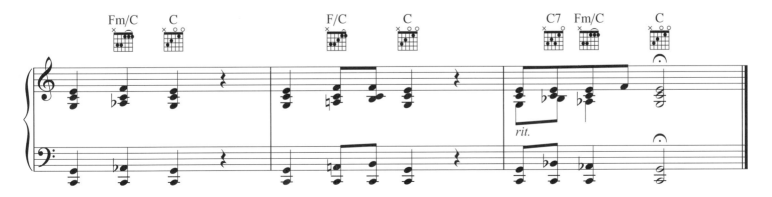

MISTLETOE

Words and Music by JUSTIN BIEBER,
NASRI ATWEH and ADAM MESSINGER

Easy Reggae feel

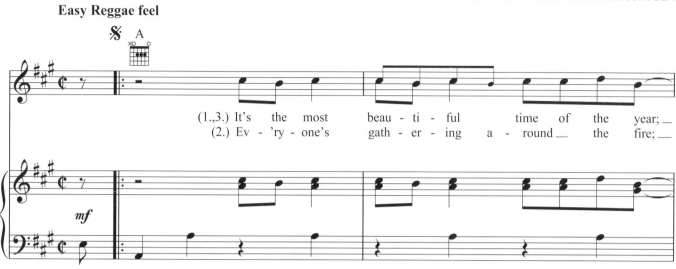

(1.,3.) It's the most beau-ti-ful time of the year; __
(2.) Ev-'ry-one's gath-er-ing a-round __ the fire; __

__ lights fill the streets, spread-ing so much cheer. __ I should be
__ chest-nuts __ roast-ing like a hot Ju-ly. ___ I should be

play-ing in the win-ter snow, __ but I'm-a be un-der the mis-tle-toe. __
chill-in' with my folks, I know, __ but I'm-a be un-der the mis-tle-toe. __

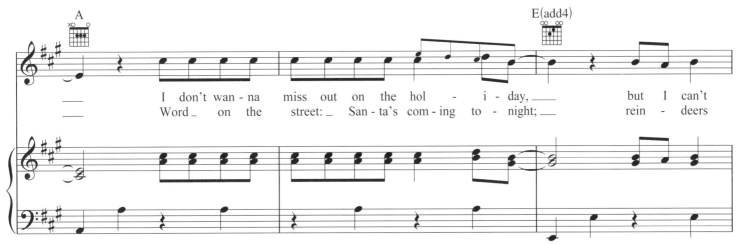

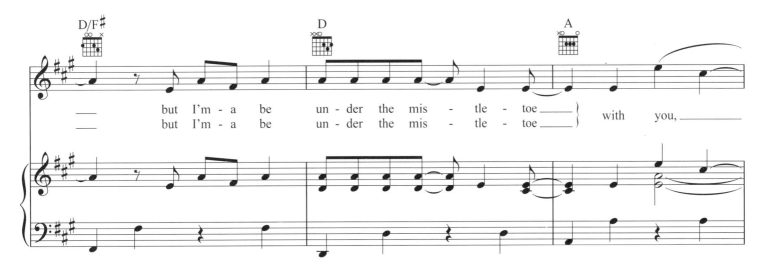

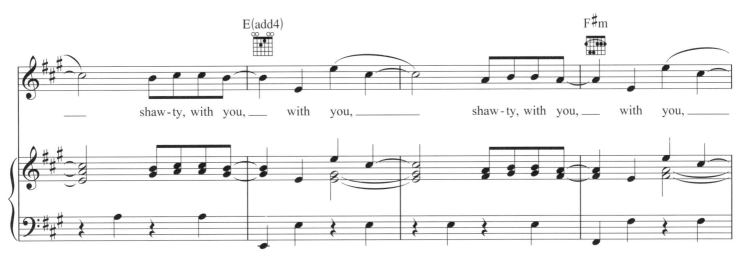

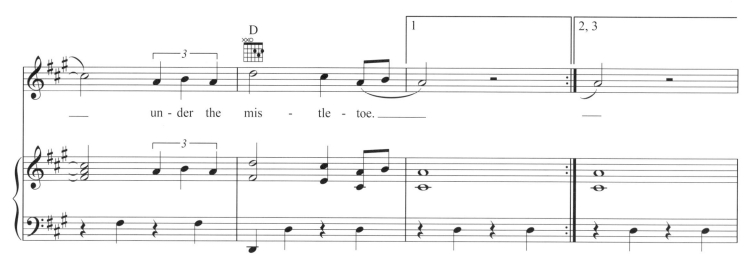

un - der the mis - tle - toe.

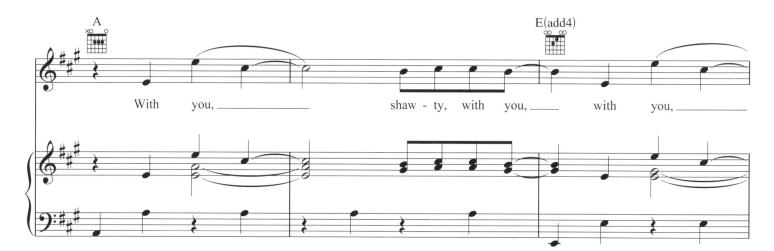

With you, _____ shaw - ty, with you, _____ with you, _____

shaw - ty, with you, _____ with you, _____ un - der the

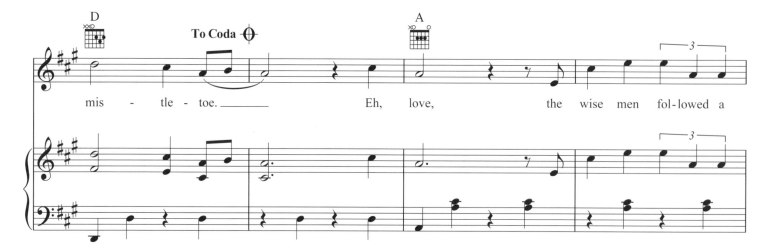

mis - tle - toe. _____ Eh, love, the wise men fol - lowed a

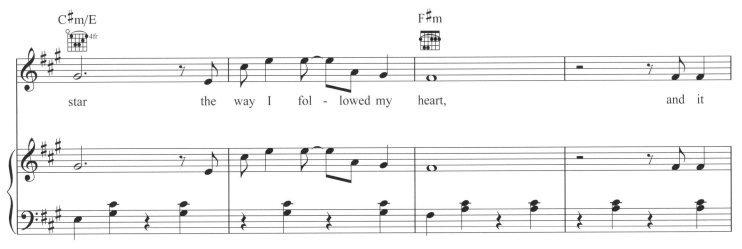

star   the way I fol - lowed my heart,   and it

led me to a mir - a - cle.___ Eh, love,   don't you buy___ me noth -

ing,   'cause I ain't feel - ing one thing: your

D.S. al Coda
(take 2nd ending)

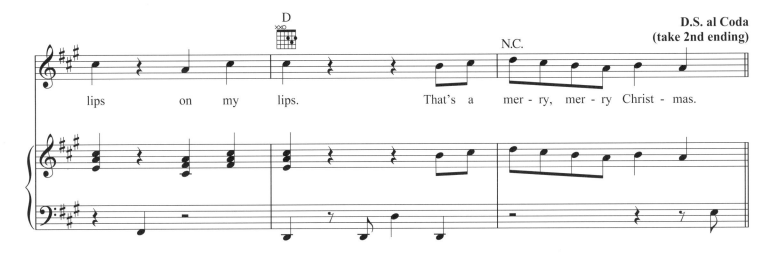

lips   on my lips.   That's a mer - ry, mer - ry Christ - mas.

CODA

Kiss me un - der - neath the

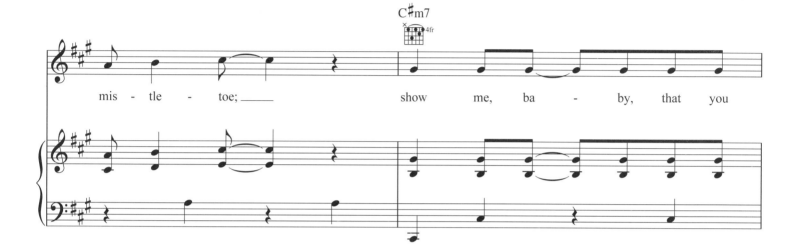

mis - tle - toe; _____ show me, ba - by, that you

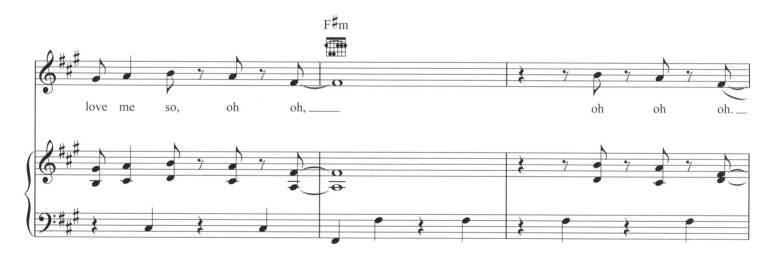

love me so, oh oh, _____ oh oh oh. _____

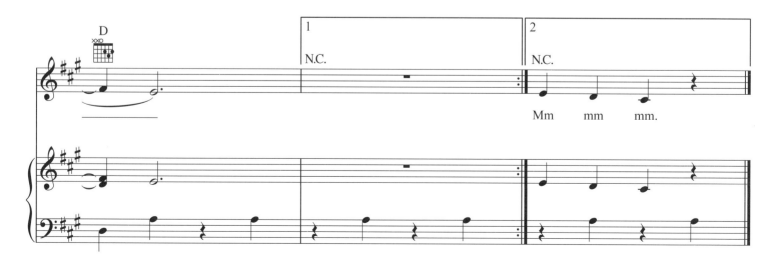

Mm mm mm.

SOMETHING ABOUT DECEMBER

Words and Music by CHRISTINA PERRI,
NICK PERRI and DAVID HODGES

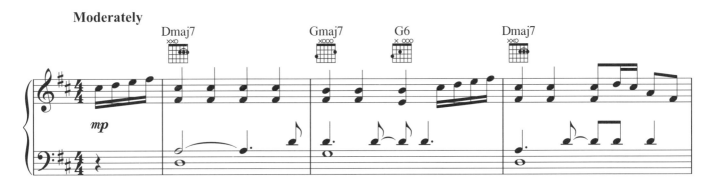

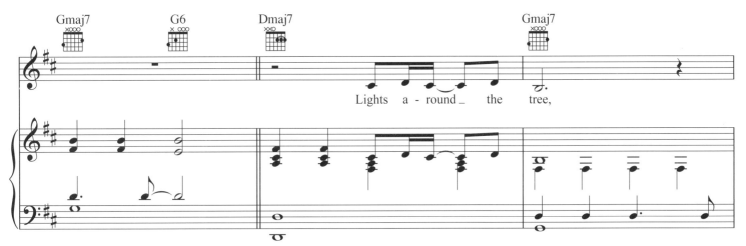

Lights a-round the tree,

Ma-ma's whis - tl-ing. ___ Takes me back a - gain. ___ There's some-thing 'bout De -

cem - ber. We're hang-ing mis - tle - toe

and hop-ing that __ it snows. I close my eyes and then I can still re-

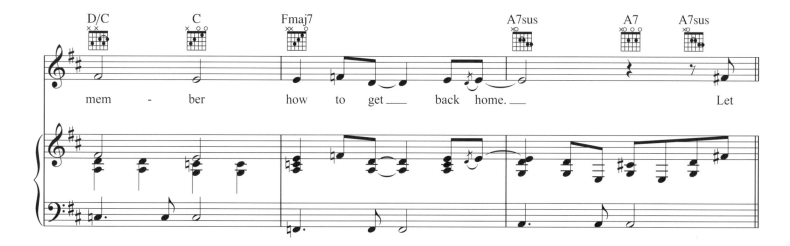

mem - ber how to get ___ back home. ___ Let

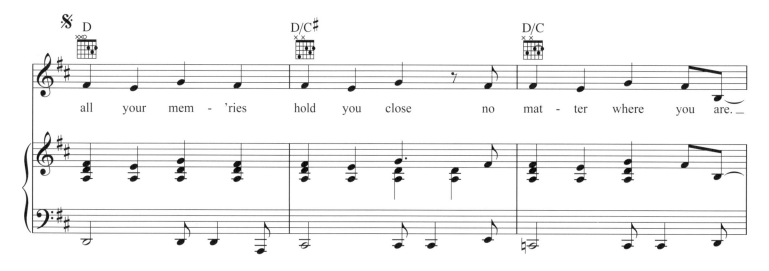

all your mem - 'ries hold you close no mat - ter where you are. __

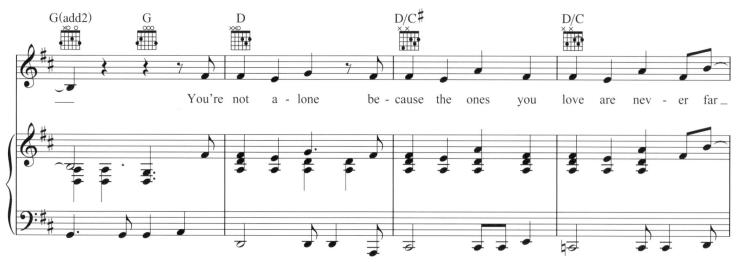

__ You're not a - lone be - cause the ones you love are nev - er far __

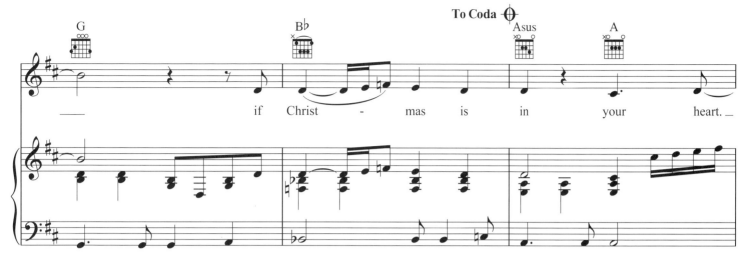

if Christ - mas is in your heart.

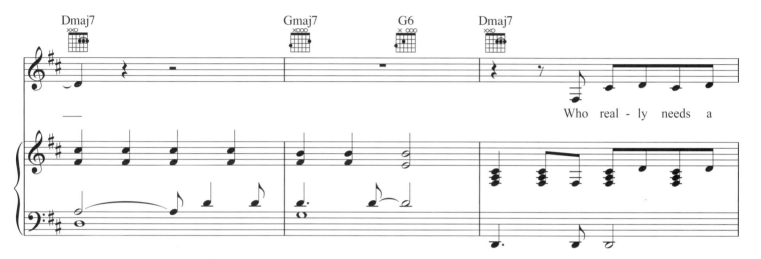

Who real - ly needs a

gift when love is meant _ to give? _ I can still re -

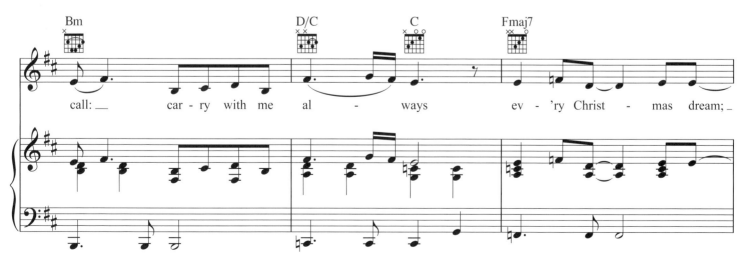

call: _ car - ry with me al - ways ev - 'ry Christ - mas dream; _

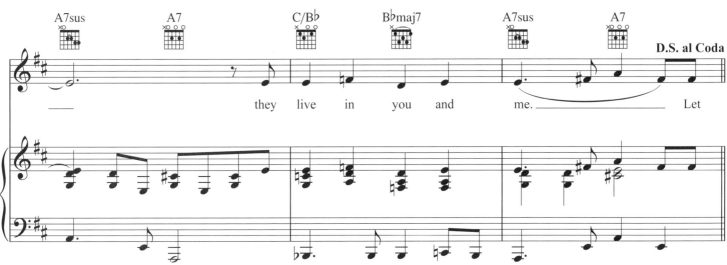

they live in you and me. _____ Let

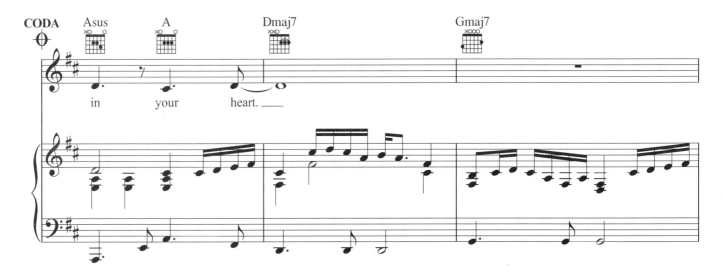

in your heart. ___

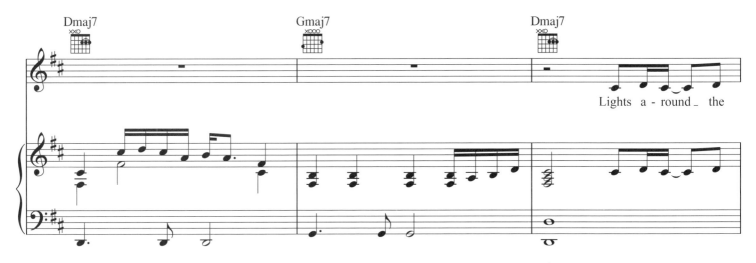

Lights a - round _ the

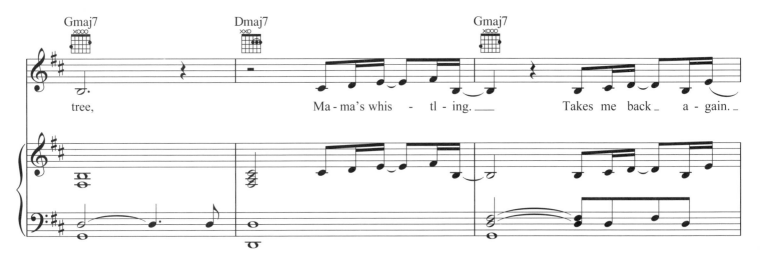

tree,   Ma - ma's whis - tl - ing. ___   Takes me back _ a - gain. _

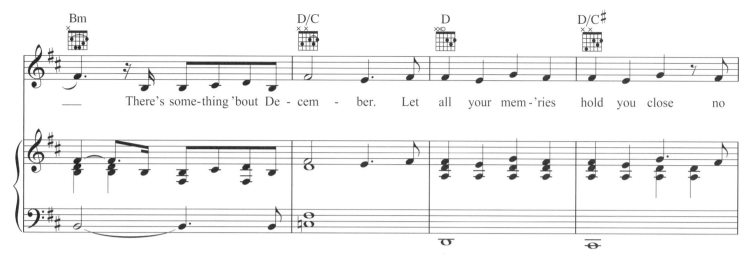

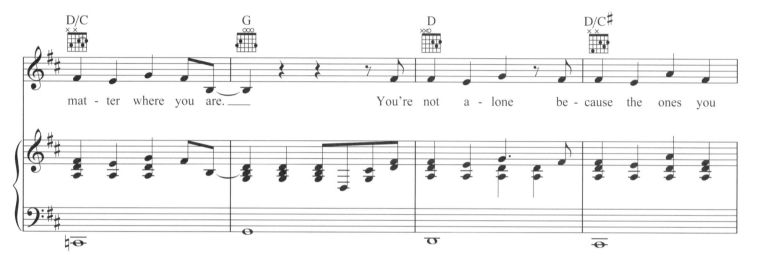

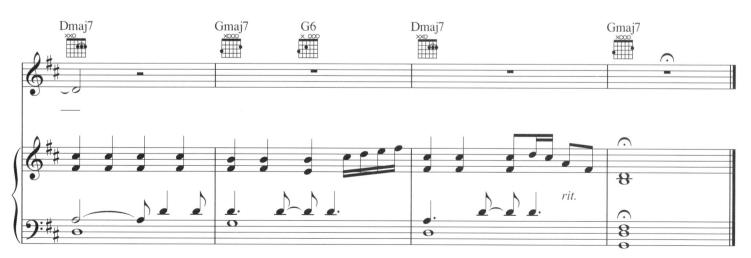

NOEL

Words and Music by MATT REDMAN,
CHRIS TOMLIN and ED CASH

Moderate Ballad

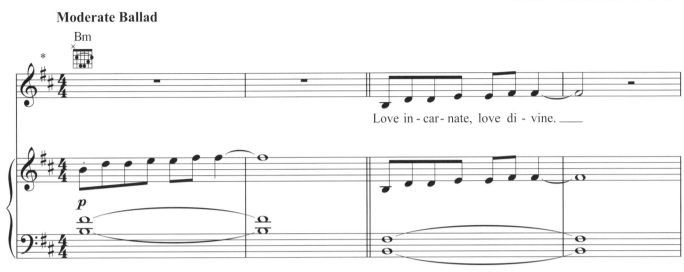

Love in-car-nate, love di-vine. ____

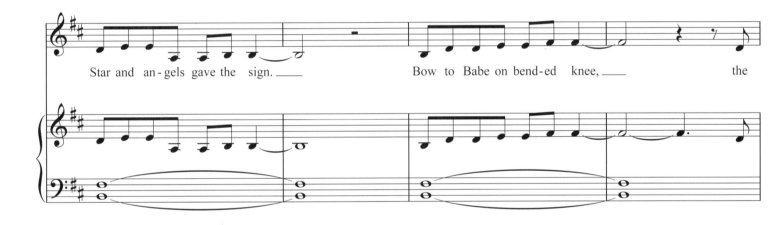

Star and an-gels gave the sign. ____ Bow to Babe on bend-ed knee, ____ the

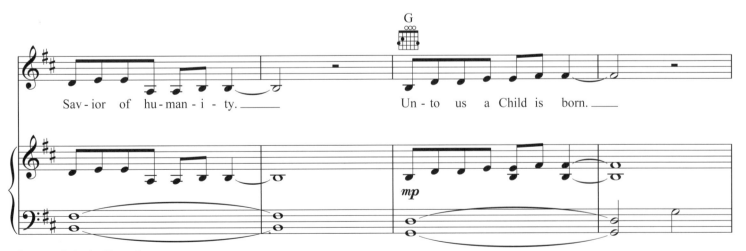

Sav-ior of hu-man-i-ty. ____ Un-to us a Child is born. ____

* Recorded a half step lower.

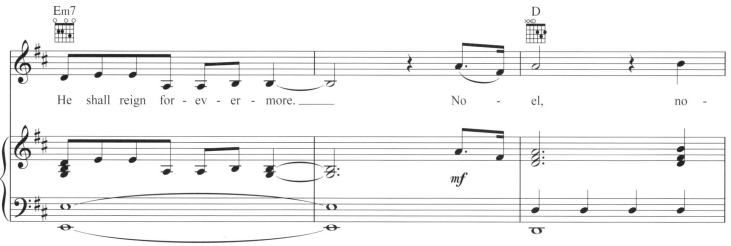

He shall reign for - ev - er - more. _____ No - el, no -

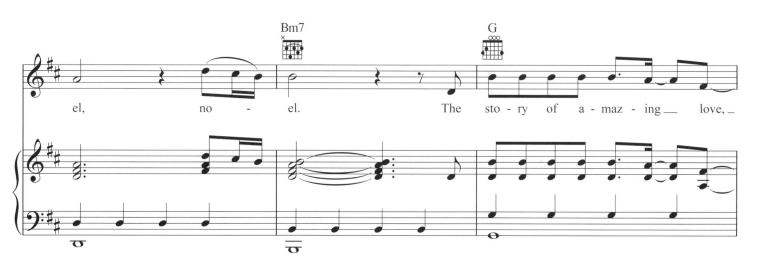

el. Come and see what God has _ done. _____ No -

el, no - el. The sto - ry of a - maz - ing _ love, _

_____ the light of the world _ giv - en for us, _____ no - el. _____

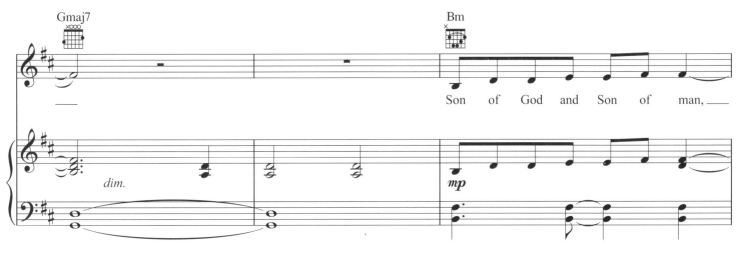

Son of God and Son of man, there be-fore the world be-gan.

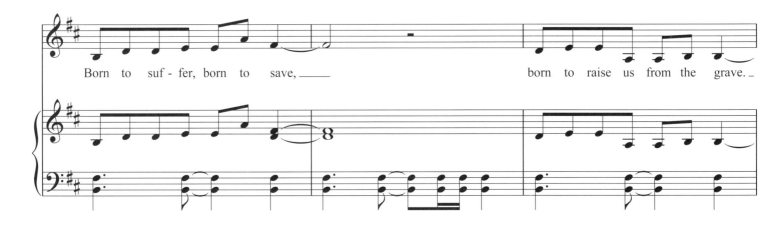

Born to suf-fer, born to save, born to raise us from the grave.

Christ, the ev-er-last-ing Lord,

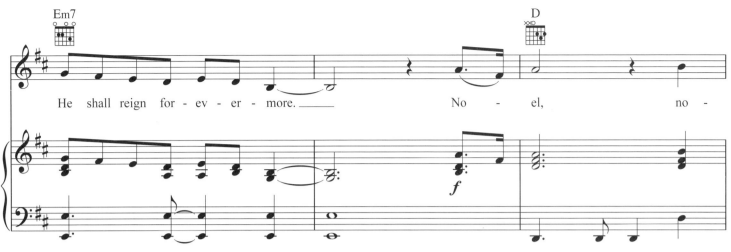

He shall reign for-ev-er-more. _____ No - el, no -

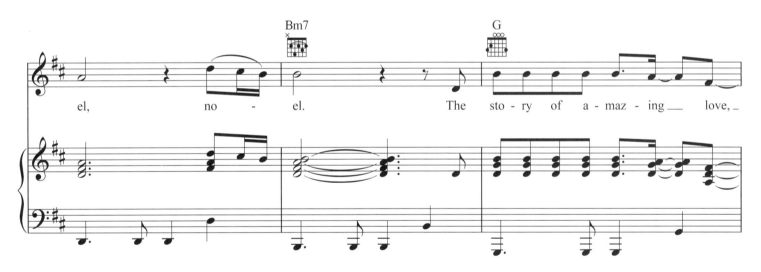

el. Come and see what God has _____ done. _____ No -

el, no - el. The sto-ry of a-maz-ing _____ love, _

_____ the light of the world _____ giv-en for us, _____ no - el. _____

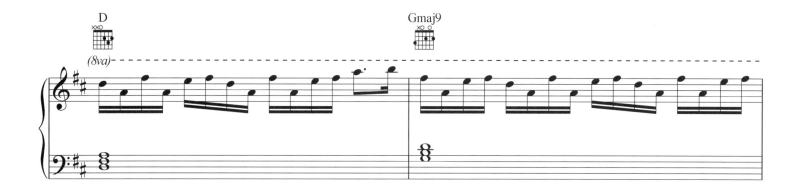

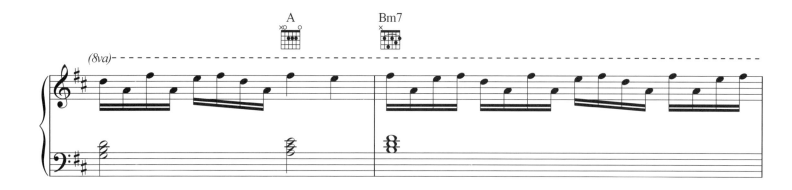

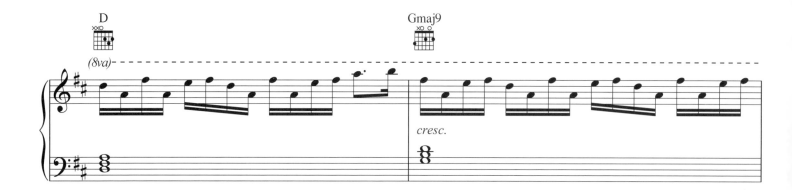

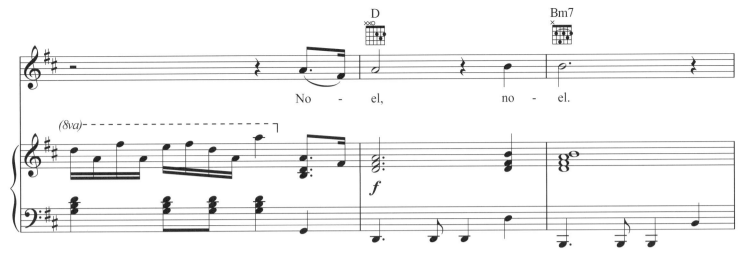

PRESENT WITHOUT A BOW

Words and Music by KACEY MUSGRAVES,
LUKE LAIRD, TODD MICHAEL BRIDGES
and AUSTIN JENKINS

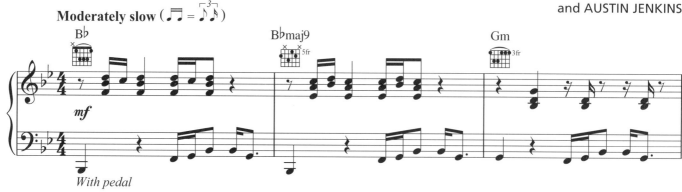

(Female:) the hol-i-day's just an-oth-er day __ that's cold, __ stand-ing all a-lone __ un-der the mis-tle - toe. __

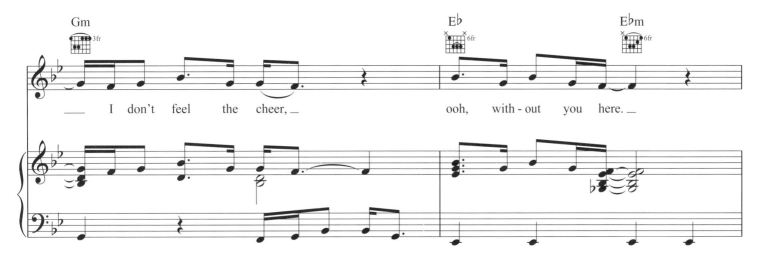

__ I don't feel the cheer, __ ooh, with-out you here. __

There's no red and white stripes on a can-dy cane. __ "Si - lent Night" __ just would-n't sound the same. __

__ Where'd the mag - ic go? __ All I know is me with-out you is like a pres-ent with-out __ a bow. __

Ooh.

Male: Be-fore we know, the wreath will come down.

The halls won't be decked; there'll be ____ no snow on the ground.

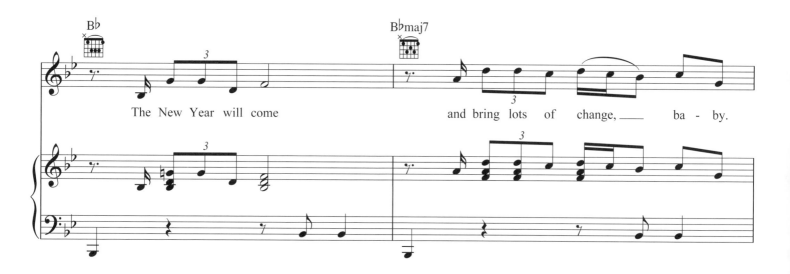

The New Year will come and bring lots of change, ____ ba - by.

And if I'm not___ with you, girl,_____ sip-ping on cham-pagne..._____

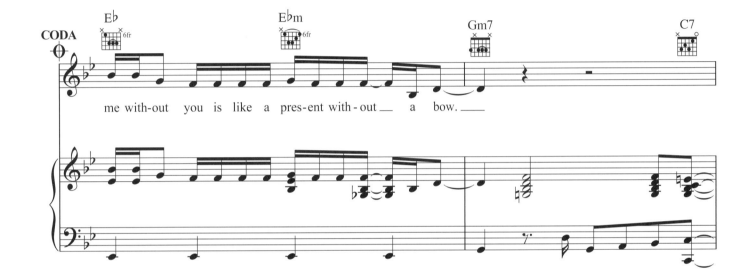

me with-out you is like a pres-ent with-out___ a bow.___

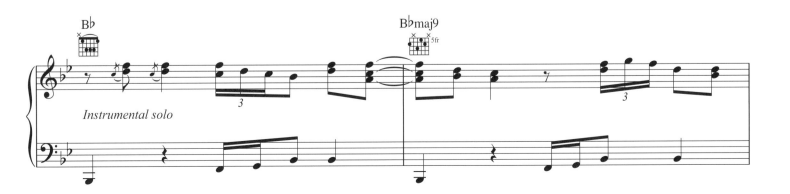

Instrumental solo

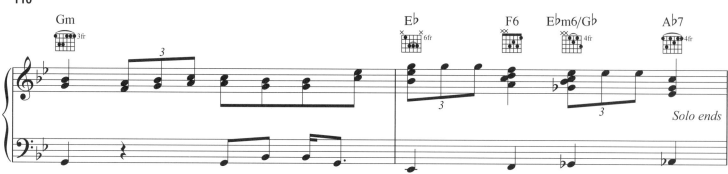

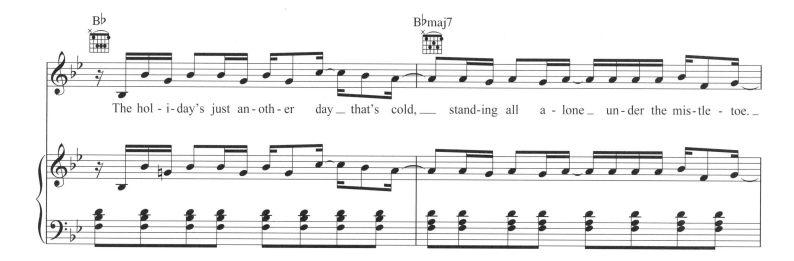

The hol - i - day's just an - oth - er day __ that's cold, __ stand - ing all a - lone __ un - der the mis - tle - toe. __

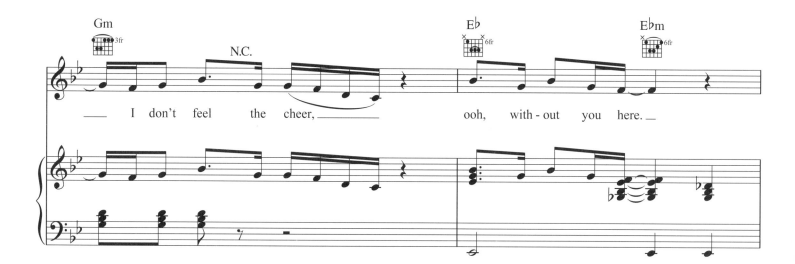

__ I don't feel the cheer, __ ooh, with - out you here. __

There's no red and white stripes on a can - dy cane. __ "Si - lent Night" __ just would - n't sound the same. __

_____ Where'd the mag - ic go? _____ All I know is me with-out you is like a pres-ent with-out _____ a bow. _____

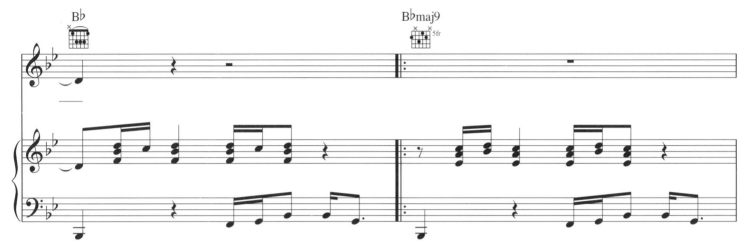

Repeat and Fade

(Male:) Me with-out you is like a pres-ent with-out _____ a bow,

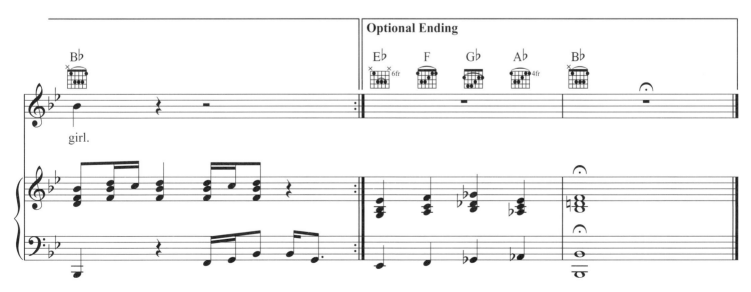

girl.

Optional Ending

SANTA TELL ME

Words and Music by SAVAN KOTECHA,
ILYA and ARIANA GRANDE

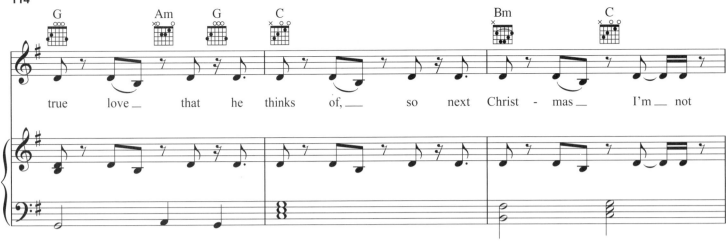

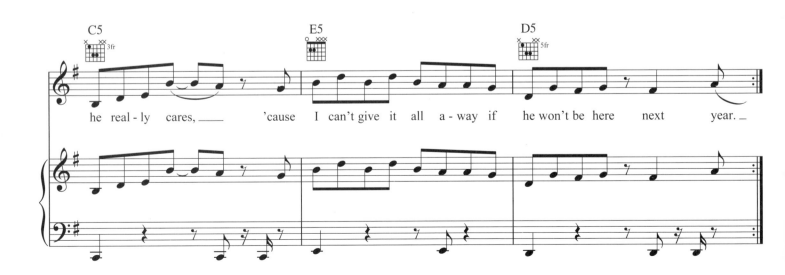

Oh, I wan - na have him be - side __ me, like, oh, __

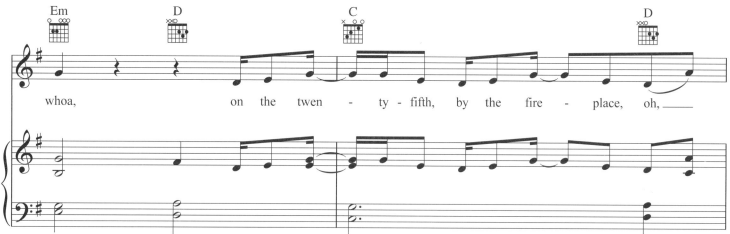

whoa, on the twen - ty - fifth, by the fire - place, oh, __

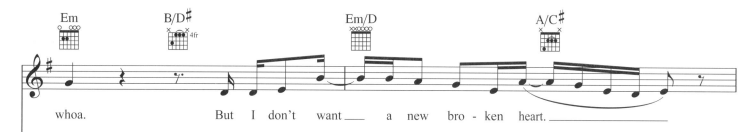

whoa. But I don't want __ a new bro - ken heart. __

This year __ I've got to __ be smart. __ Oh __

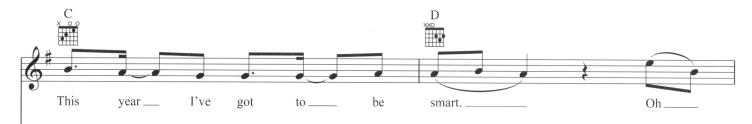

ba -
(San - ta, tell me.) by. (San - ta, tell me.) If he won't be,

if he won't be _____ here. _____
(San - ta, tell me.) (San - ta, tell me, oh yeah.) _

San - ta, tell me if you're real - ly there. _____ Don't make me fall in love a - gain if
(Lead vocal ad lib.)

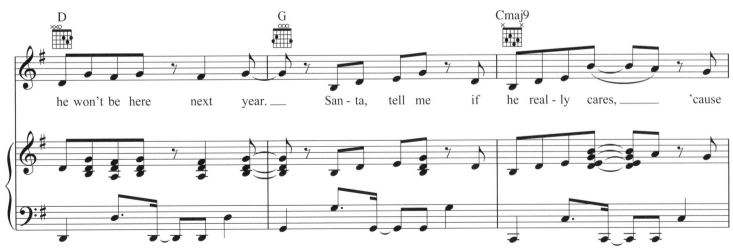

he won't be here next year. _____ San - ta, tell me if he real - ly cares, _____ 'cause

SNOWMAN

Words and Music by GREG KURSTIN
and SIA FURLER

Recorded a half step lower.

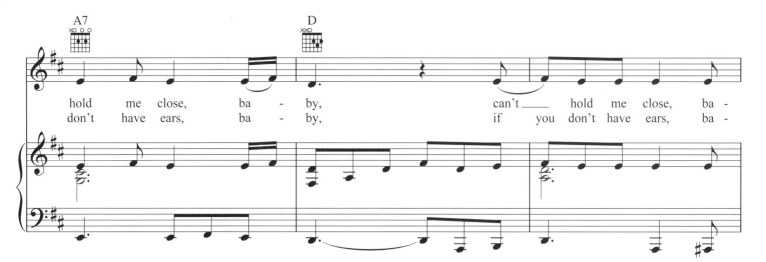

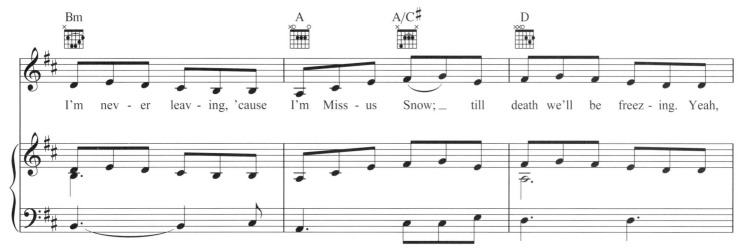

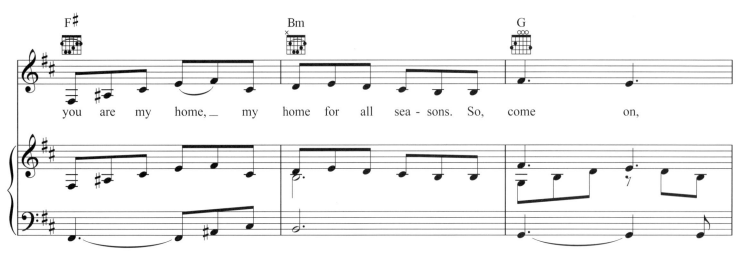

you are my home,__ my home for all sea - sons. So, come on,

let's go. Let's go be - low ze - ro and hide from the sun. I

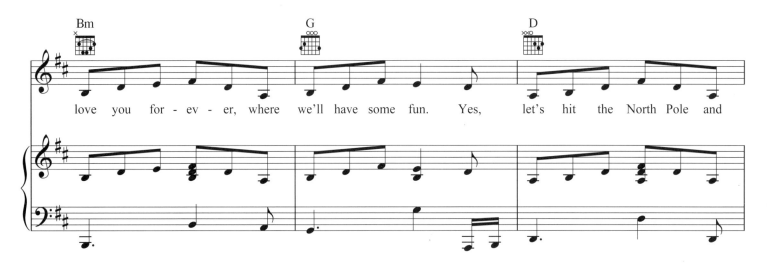

love you for - ev - er, where we'll have some fun. Yes, let's hit the North Pole and

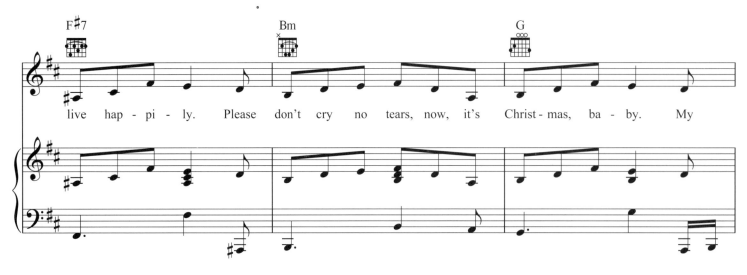

live hap - pi - ly. Please don't cry no tears, now, it's Christ - mas, ba - by. My

snow - man ___ and ___ me, _____ hey. _____

My snow - man ___ and ___ me, _____

ba - by. _____

Don't cry, ___

UNDERNEATH THE TREE

Words and Music by KELLY CLARKSON
and GREG KURSTIN

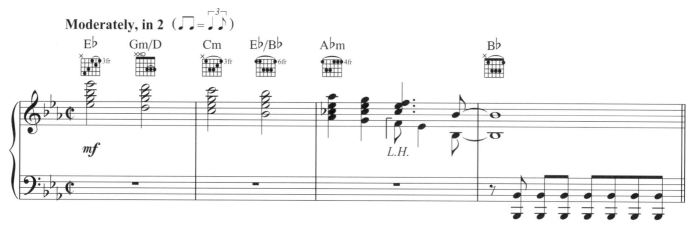

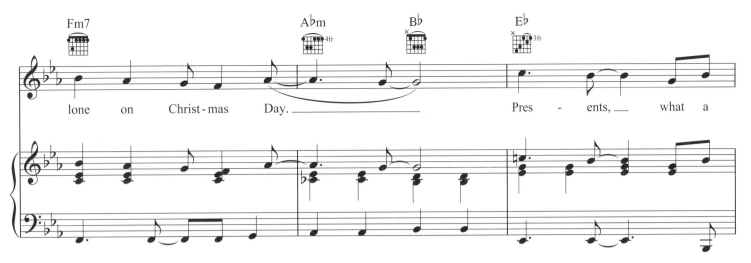

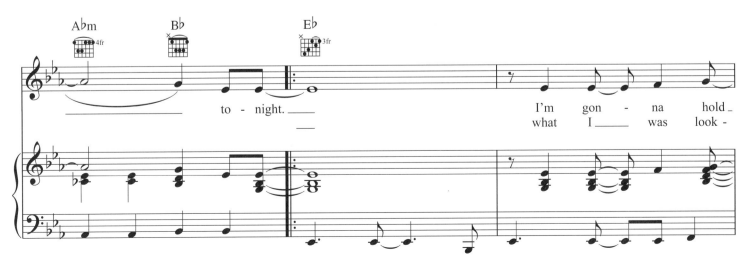

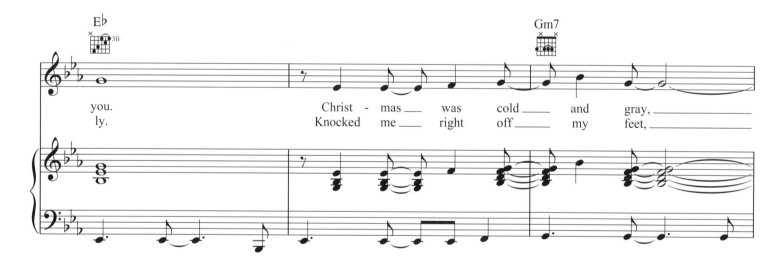

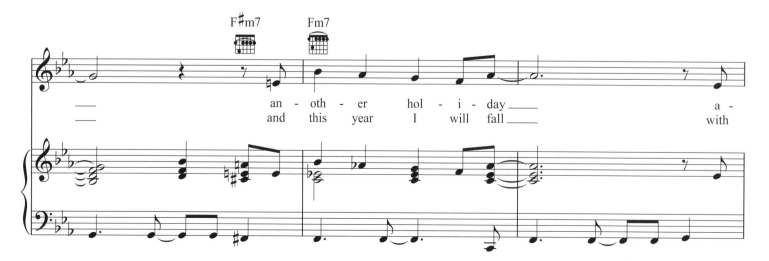

lone to cel - e - brate. _____ But then ____ one day, ___
no wor - ries at all. _____ 'Cause you ____ are near ___

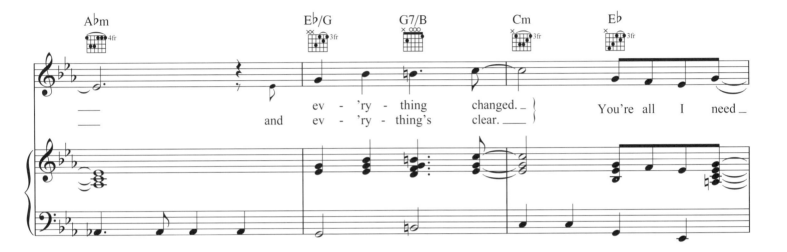

___ ev - 'ry - thing changed. You're all I need ___
___ and ev - 'ry - thing's clear. ___

un - der - neath the tree. ___ You're here ___
where you should be. ___

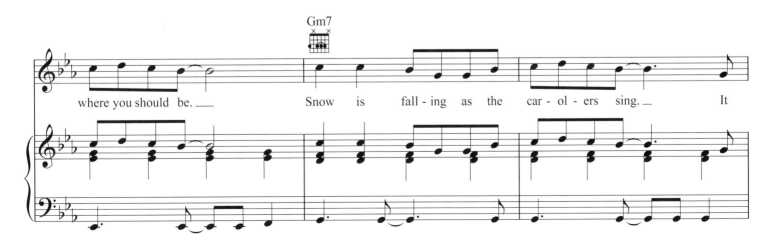

Snow is fall - ing as the car - ol - ers sing. ___ It

just was-n't the same ___ a - lone on Christ-mas Day. __

Pres - ents, __ what a beau-ti-ful sight. __

Don't mean a thing if you ain't hold-in' me tight. __ You're all that I need __

___ un - der - neath the tree. ___ I've found __

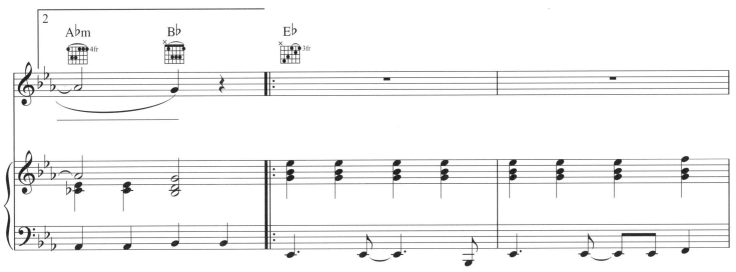

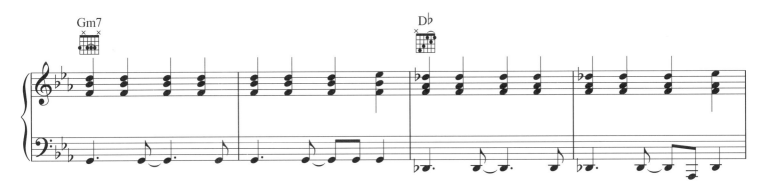

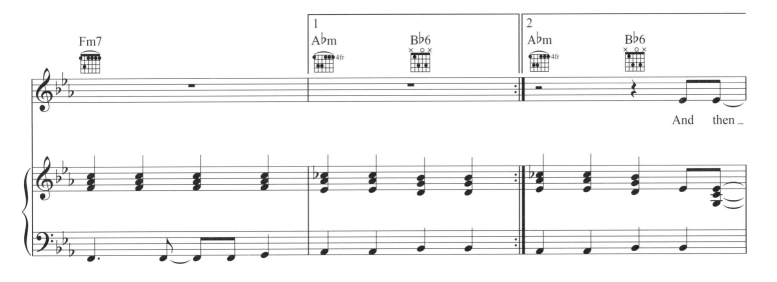

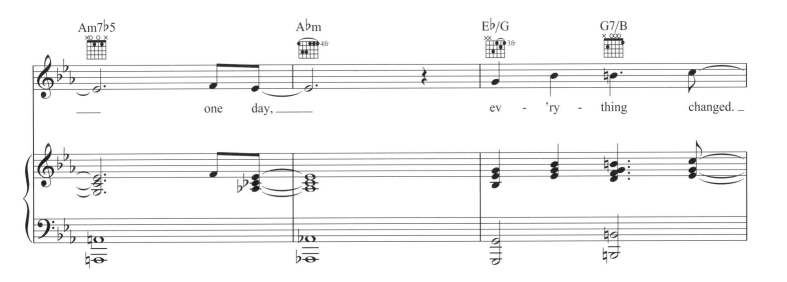

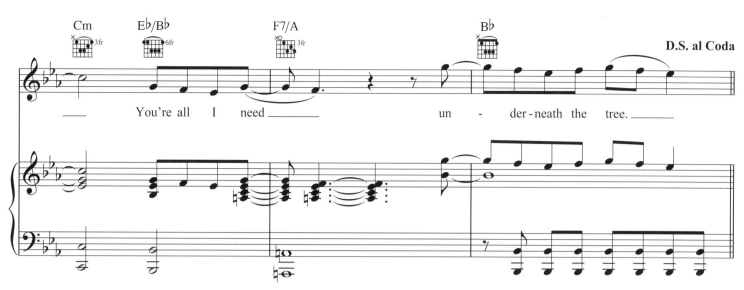

You're all I need _____ un - der-neath the tree. _____

D.S. al Coda

CODA

to - night. _____

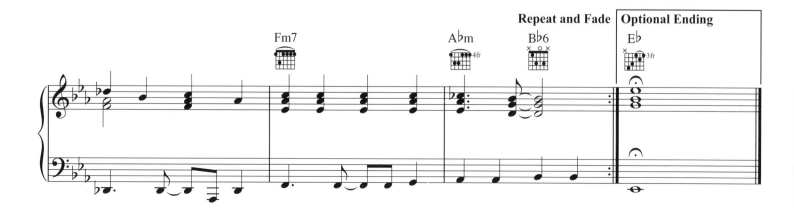

Repeat and Fade | Optional Ending